1, 2, and 3 John: Multiple Readings, Deconstructing Constructions

T&T CLARK STUDY GUIDES TO THE NEW TESTAMENT

Series Editor:
Tat-siong Benny Liew, College of the Holy Cross, USA

Other titles in the series include:
1 & 2 Thessalonians: An Introduction and Study Guide
1 Peter: An Introduction and Study Guide
2 Corinthians: An Introduction and Study Guide
Colossians: An Introduction and Study Guide
Ephesians: An Introduction and Study Guide
Galatians: An Introduction and Study Guide
Hebrews: An Introduction and Study Guide
James: An Introduction and Study Guide
John: An Introduction and Study Guide
Luke: An Introduction and Study Guide
Mark: An Introduction and Study Guide
Matthew: An Introduction and Study Guide
Philemon: An Introduction and Study Guide
Philippians: An Introduction and Study Guide
Romans: An Introduction and Study Guide
The Acts of the Apostles: An Introduction and Study Guide
The Letters of Jude and Second Peter: An Introduction and Study Guide

T&T CLARK STUDY GUIDES TO THE OLD TESTAMENT

Amos: An Introduction and Study Guide
1 & 2 Kings: An Introduction and Study Guide
1 & 2 Samuel: An Introduction and Study Guide
Daniel: An Introduction and Study Guide
Ecclesiastes: An Introduction and Study Guide
Exodus: An Introduction and Study Guide
Ezra-Nehemiah: An Introduction and Study Guide
Haggai, Zechariah and Malachi: An Introduction and Study Guide Isaiah:
An Introduction and Study Guide
Jeremiah: An Introduction and Study Guide
Job: An Introduction and Study Guide
Joel, Obadiah, Habakkuk, Zephaniah: An Introduction and Study Guide
Joshua: An Introduction and Study Guide
Leviticus: An Introduction and Study Guide
Numbers: An Introduction and Study Guide
Proverbs: And Introduction and Study Guide
Psalms: An Introduction and Study Guide
Song of Songs: An Introduction and Study Guide
Genesis: An Introduction and Study Guide

1, 2, and 3 John: Multiple Readings, Deconstructing Constructions

An Introduction and Study Guide

Warren Carter

t&tclark

LONDON · NEW YORK · OXFORD · NEW DELHI · SYDNEY

T&T CLARK
Bloomsbury Publishing Plc
50 Bedford Square, London, WC1B 3DP, UK
1385 Broadway, New York, NY 10018, USA
29 Earlsfort Terrace, Dublin 2, Ireland

BLOOMSBURY, T&T CLARK and the T&T Clark logo are trademarks
of Bloomsbury Publishing Plc

First published in Great Britain 2024

A catalogue record for this book is available from the British Library.

A catalog record for this book is available from the Library of Congress.

ISBN: HB: 978-0-5677-0420-7
         PB: 978-0-5677-0421-4
         ePDF: 978-0-5677-0422-1
         eBook: 978-0-5677-0423-8

Series: T&T Clark's Study Guides to the New Testament

Typeset by RefineCatch Ltd, Bungay, Suffolk
Printed and bound in Great Britain

To find out more about our authors and books, visit www.bloomsbury.com
and sign up for our newsletters.

Contents

Part 3 2 and 3 John

Introduction

The nine chapters of this study of 1, 2, and 3 John (the Johannine Writings) are organized in three parts.

Part 1 comprises three chapters. Chapter 1 highlights how little we know about six aspects of these writings particularly related to their origins. Chapters 2 and 3 discuss two different approaches to the interpretation of the writings. One understands them as part of a Johannine tradition in which a schism is central (Chapter 2; Brown). The other approach (my preference) understands them as independent writings and not experiencing schism (Chapter 3; Lieu).

Part 2 focuses on 1 John and comprises four chapters. Chapter 4 discusses the puzzling issue of 1 John's structure or organization, and emphasizes the conceptual and rhetorical links drawing the small units together. Chapter 5 engages the debate as to whether 1 John is a polemical or pastoral writing. Developing the latter designation, Chapter 6 argues that 1 John functions as epideictic rhetoric to confirm the recipients' identity and way of life. Chapter 7 outlines some of the theological understandings that underpin the writing's pastoral work.

Part 3 discusses the two letters of 2 John (Chapter 8) and 3 John (Chapter 9).

I cite translations from the New Revised Standard Version unless otherwise indicated. Given the nature of this series, I have employed limited endnotes and bibliographic entries. A much larger body of scholarly work encountered over the years informs the material offered here. I have referenced the most relevant.

I appreciate the invitation of Dr. Benny Liew to contribute to this series, and the helpful comments from Professor Judith Lieu on Chapter 3.

Part 1

Locating Readings of 1, 2, and 3 John

1

Matters We Don't Know about 1, 2, and 3 John

The three brief writings known as 1 John, 2 John, and 3 John are tucked away near the end of the New Testament. First John is often known for two verses, an assurance of forgiveness often declared in worship services, and an emphasis on love. So we read:

> If we confess our sins, he who is faithful and just will forgive us our sins and cleanse us from all unrighteousness.
>
> (1 Jn 1:9)

> Beloved, let us love one another, because love is from God; everyone who loves is born of God and knows God. Whoever does not love does not know God, for God is love.
>
> (1 Jn 4:7-8)

Yet a number of aspects of these documents, known as the Johannine Letters or the Johannine Epistles, are not clearcut. For example, while 2 and 3 John employ the form of a letter, 1 John does not. In light of this, I will refer throughout to 1, 2, and 3 John as "writings" or "documents" rather than "letters."

In this chapter, I discuss six aspects of these writings about which we have no definitive explanations or answers. Surprisingly, we do not know 1) who wrote them; 2) the relationship of the three writings to each other and to the Gospel of John; 3) the order in which the three writings were written; 4) when they were written; 5) where they were written; and 6) to whom they were written.

Author? Authors?

The New Testament canon calls these writings 1, 2, and 3 John respectively. Yet none of the documents explicitly identifies its author with the name John. Dionysius of Alexandria observed this absence in the third century (Eusebius, *Hist. eccl.* 7.25.7-11). Moreover, the documents do not give any name at all to their authors; they prefer anonymity. Both 2 John and 3 John claim to be written by "the elder," but that elder is not named. More accurately, perhaps we should think of them as Non-Johns.

While 1 John does not identify its author by name, its opening four verses might suggest multiple authors.

> We declare to you what was from the beginning, what we have heard, what we have seen with our eyes, what we have looked at and touched with our hands, concerning the word of life . . . We are writing these things so that our joy may be complete.
>
> (1 Jn 1:1, 4)

What is the meaning of the plural pronouns "we" and "our"? Do they suggest a committee and/or a community as authors for 1 John? Or does a single author use the plural "we" to refer to a tradition that s/he is upholding and with which s/he aligns themself? Or does a single author initially use the "royal we" to assert authority over the readers/hearers whom the author (perhaps a male?) addresses as "(my little) children" (1 Jn 2:1; also 2:18, 28; 3:7, 18; 4:4; 5:21). This kinship language might express a loving relationship and even a communal identity of a family or household presided over by a parental-patriarchal figure. Yet it certainly asserts a power relationship of domination or "power over" in constructing the readers/audience as infantilized subjects subject to the writer's authority.[1]

At the beginning of Chapter 2, this plural language becomes the singular "I": "I am writing these things." The document uses this first person singular form ten more times in Chapter 2 and once more in 5:13. This narrowing from the plural to singular is strange. Perhaps it suggests that, having aligned himself with a particular tradition or community and asserted his authority, the unnamed individual author now feels free to make his own contribution.

---

[1] R. S. Sugirtharajah, "The First, Second, and Third Letters of John." In F. Segovia and R. S. Sugirtharajah (eds.), *A Postcolonial Commentary on the New Testament Writings* (London: T & T Clark, 2007), 413–23, esp. 417–18.

The author or authors of 2 and 3 John also do not identify themselves by name. Each one authoritatively employs the first person singular "I" form (2 Jn 5, 12; 3 Jn 13 [2x]), and declares his hopes to visit his audience (2 Jn 12; 3 Jn 14). Is the "elder" that 2 and 3 John claim as authors the same person, or two separate figures using this common title? Does one letter copy the title from the other? And did either/both of them also write 1 John? We simply do not know.

And the term "elder" is ambiguous. It can have a literal meaning that signifies an old man. And it can also denote a position of ecclesial leadership (so 1 Tim. 5:17, 19; Tit. 1:5; Jas 5:14; 1 Pet. 5:1-5). At the outset of these letters, does it signify the age of the authors or does it assert a position of leadership and authority—or both? Like 1 John, both letters construct their audiences as a household. By calling them "children," the writer-elder asserts authority over them (2 Jn 1, 4, 13; 3 Jn 4).

Since the writings do not use the name "John," how did it become linked to these writings? And since we know of several characters named John in the early churches, which John might be in view? Some speculation about the writings' author/s in the second century posited an author named John who was not the apostle John. An early church figure called Papias made this identification. We know about Papias not directly from his own writings but from the fourth-century Christian writer Eusebius. Writing several centuries after Papias died, Eusebius says that Papias referred to an elder called John from whom Papias learned sayings of the Lord (Eusebius, *Hist. eccl.* 3.39). This John, according to Papias, is not John the apostle but John the elder. And Eusebius says that Papias employed material from "the former letter of John" (*Hist. eccl.* 3.39.17). The wording "former" suggests that Papias knew of at least two letters associated with this "John."

Yet Papias' opinion was not shared by everyone. Others in the second century asserted that John the Apostle and disciple of Jesus *was* the author of not only the Gospel of John but also these writings. Around 180 CE, for example, Irenaeus makes this link (*Adv. Her.* 1.16.3-8). In his attack on those he considered to have wandered from orthodox thinking, he cites from the Gospel, 1 John, and 2 John. He introduces the citations as being from "John the Lord's disciple." He cites John 20:31 ("But these things are written that you might believe …"). Then Irenaeus says, referring to John the apostle, "in his Epistle he has borne this witness" and cites 1 John 2:18-19, 21-2 ("Little children it is the last hour…. This is the Antichrist"). And subsequently, Irenaeus introduces further citations from John "his disciple in his aforementioned epistle …". Irenaeus cites 1 John 4:1-3, 5:1, and 2 John 7–8

("Many deceivers have gone out into the world …"). Irenaeus asserts that the apostle John wrote the Gospel of John and 1 and 2 John. Into recent times, some scholars have continued to claim Johannine apostolic authorship of these writings. Yet if John the apostle were the author, it is surprising that he did not assert his authority over his recipients by putting his name on the writings.

Irenaeus' claim, though, did not convince everyone. While Eusebius (*Hist. eccl.* 7.25.6) reports that others such as Dionysius of Alexandria (*c.* 250) affirmed the apostle to be the author of John's gospel and the writings (but not Revelation), he also attests that some held a different opinion on the author of 2 and 3 John. He reports that Origen, in the early third century, declares that John the apostle wrote the Gospel of John and Revelation, plus a letter (probably 1 John). But Origen and others are doubtful about the apostle's authorship of 2 and 3 John. He says, "there may also be a second and third, but not all say these are genuine" (Eusebius, *Hist. eccl.* 6.25.9-10).

Irenaeus' assertions date from some sixty to eighty years after the likely composition of the three writings around 120 CE. He makes claims about the writings in the context of arguing against his opponents. He appeals to writings that he deems to be authoritative by linking them to apostles and disciples of Jesus. His argument is theological and ecclesial, not historical. It is designed to promote what Irenaeus and others considered to be acceptable beliefs and writings. The claims are not based on historical evidence and so do not provide reliable or accurate historical evidence for identifying the actual author or authors of 1, 2, and 3 John.

It is a matter of honesty to say that we do not know who wrote any of these documents.

Yet we get some idea of how the writer of 1 John constructs himself. He employs a variety of techniques to assert his authority over his recipients whom he addresses either patronizingly or affectionately as "children." He claims the authenticity of his message (1 Jn 1:1-3). He claims divine sanction for himself and his message (1 Jn 4:6). He works hard throughout to establish a binary or dualism with himself allied with God and the recipients, and opposed to the devil (1 Jn 3:8-10). He claims his Christological understandings of Jesus's incarnation and atoning death as normative, and has no tolerance for any diversity of belief or dissent from these understandings. He identifies opposing entities and forces which he maligns with derogatory terms such as "antichrists," "false prophets," "liars," "children of the devil," and "deceivers," He gives them no voice, hospitality, or divine favor. He expects his addressees to live faithfully to the truth and to the divine commandments that he sets forth, especially love for other believers. He constructs himself as the defender and promoter of truth, and deeply committed to maintaining the loyal obedience of those whom he addresses.

In discussing 2 and 3 John in Chapters 8 and 9, we will gain some sense of the elders who write those letters.

The Relationship of these Writings to the Gospel of John

The relationship/s between the four NT writings that bear the name "John"—Gospel of John, 1, 2, and 3 John—has/have perplexed interpreters. The writings share some commonalities in language and themes, yet there are also significant differences. Any understanding of the relationships among the four must account for both the commonalities and the differences.

One claim has been that the Gospel of John was written first and supplies the language and themes for 1, 2, and 3 John. Some scholars have spent a lot of time counting the words used in the writings and comparing them to the numbers of words used in John's Gospel. The idea has been that high levels of shared language would indicate a common author or common tradition with the writings depending on the Gospel.

Yet the data is much more ambiguous. In the following examples of Greek words, remember that the Gospel is approximately three times longer than the three writings with twenty-one chapters, while the combined three writings total only seven chapters.[2]

- The verb "to love:" Writings 31x; Gospel 34x;
- The noun "love:" Writings 21x; Gospel 7x;
- The verb "to live:" Writings 1x; Gospel 16x;
- The noun "life:" Writings 13x; Gospel 37x;
- The noun "God:" Writings 66x; Gospel 80x;
- The noun "Father;" Writings 18x; Gospel 34x;
- The noun "Jesus;" Writings 14x; Gospel 239x;
- The noun "son;" Writings 24x; Gospel 57x;
- The noun "Christ;" Writings 12x; Gospel 19x;

---

[2] I derive the numbers from the lists of Greek terms in A. E. Brooke, *The Johannine Epistles.* ICC (Edinburgh: T&T Clark, 1912), 229–42.

- The three nouns "(little) children:" Writings 19x; Gospel 7x;
- The noun "person/human being:" Writings 1x; Gospel 59x;
- The verb "to witness;" Writings 10x; Gospel 33x;
- The verb "confess;" Writings 6x; Gospel 4x;
- The adjective "evil;" Writings 8x; Gospel 3x;
- The verb "send;" Writings 3x; Gospel 28x;
- The noun "light;" Writings 6x; Gospel 22x;
- The nouns "darkness;" Writings 6x; Gospel 9x;
- The noun "water;" Writings 4x; Gospel 25x;
- The noun "commandment:" Writings 18x; Gospel 11x;
- The noun "truth;" Writings 20x; Gospel 25x;
- The verb "believe/have faith;" Writings 9x; Gospel 94x;
- The conjunction "so that/in order to;" Writings 28x; Gospel 145x.

This random selection highlights some common vocabulary that the three writings and Gospel of John share. It identifies some terms emphasized more in the Gospel than the writings ("live;" "Jesus;" "water;" "send;" "believe") and some terms stressed more, proportionally, in the writings ("to love/love;" "God;" "little children;" "confess;" "evil;" "commandment"). A sustained analysis would highlight more instances of heightened and diminished emphases in the writings in relation to the Gospel. But even this brief selection of examples questions the claim that the three writings have a consistent literary dependence on the Gospel.

Further, there are numerous words that are prominent in the Gospel that do not occur at all in the writings. Here are a few of the prominent ones:

- The noun "glory" (17x) and the verb "glorify (22x);
- The verb "follow" (19x);
- The distinctive phrase "truly, truly" (25x);
- The verb "raise" (13x);
- The verbs "come down" (18x) and "go up" (16x);
- The verb "judge" (19x);
- The noun "Lord" (52x);
- The noun "disciple" (78x);
- The noun "heaven" (20x);
- The noun "sign" (17x);
- The noun "cross (4x) and verb "crucify" (10x).

Moreover, important words in the three writings are absent from the Gospel:

- Beloved (10x);
- Antichrist (5x);
- The verb "greet" (3x);
- Church/assembly (3x);
- Fellowship (4x);
- Means of forgiving sin/expiation (2x);
- Faithful (2x).

In these examples, words that are central to the Gospel's story of Jesus do not figure in the writings. And key words in the three writings do not occur in the Gospel. What do these data tell us? Do they point to shared or different authors? Do they indicate that the Gospel preceded the three writings, or that the three writings preceded the Gospel, or that there is no literary relationship but a common tradition? The data are complex; the latter option seems most likely.

Further, we can identify specific differences in themes between John's Gospel and 1 John. Among 1 John's emphases are themes that are either minimal in and absent from the Gospel including some eschatological motifs ("last hour," 2:18; "day of judgment,"), Jesus's atoning death ("expiation," 2:1; 4:10), antichrists and false prophets (2:18, 22; 4:1, 3), types of sinfulness (2:16-17; 3:4; 4:6; 5:16-17), the anointing of believers (2:20, 27), a less prominent role for the Spirit (4:1-6), and the absence of citations from the Hebrew Bible.

Between the Gospel and 2 John, there are only a few common themes: "truth" (2 Jn 1–4), "abiding in" (2 Jn 2, 9), Father and Son (2 Jn 3, 9), and a new commandment (2 Jn 5). There are significant differences: "the church as lady" (2 Jn 1, 5), "antichrist" (2 Jn 7) and "reward" (2 Jn 8).

Third John shares the theme of "truth" with the Gospel (3 Jn 1, 3, 4, 8, 12), yet again there are significant differences: "church" (3 Jn 6, 9, 10), "non-believers" (3 Jn 7), and "authority" (3 Jn 9).

What, then, can we say about the relationship between John's Gospel and these three documents bearing the name "John?" One approach has been to suggest that the Gospel predates the writings and the writings draw on the Gospel, mostly sharing its vocabulary and themes while also at times making some changes, emphasizing or diminishing some themes and adding new ones. We'll look at this (unlikely) approach in more detail in the next chapter.

A second interpretive approach admits we just don't know if the authors of 1, 2, and 3 John drew on John's Gospel. As this discussion shows, there are connections but also significant differences among the writings. Nor is it even clear when the writings were written in relation to each other. Was the Gospel written before the three writings and was it available to the writers? Were these three writings written first? We do not know. This second approach explains the similarities and differences among them not by positing literary interactions but by positing a flexible common worldview, tradition, themes, and vocabulary which the writers of the writings drew on freely.

This approach prefers to discuss each writing on its own terms rather than in relation to the Gospel. This appeal to a common worldview and tradition is more fluid than positing the Gospel as a written source, and so is more difficult to demonstrate in a detailed way. Its merit is that it readily accounts for commonalities and differences. We will look at this approach in more detail in Chapter 3.

The Relationship of the Three Writings to Each Other

A related "unknown" concerns the relationship of the three writings to each other. Were they written by the same author and in what order? Does the canonical sequence reflect the order in which they were written?

Interpreters have suggested a spectrum of responses to these questions. Based on the previous discussion of language and themes, it seems unlikely that one author wrote all three. Some have argued that the explicit letter form of 2 and 3 John, the shared identification of the author as "the Elder," the reference in 3 John 9 to a former letter, and the similar length of 2 and 3 John point to a common author for 2 and 3 John. This claim seems persuasive, yet there are differences between the two letters. Third John does not employ the Christological confession of 2 John 7–9. The reference in 3 John 9 to Diotrephes and 3 John 12 to Demetrius have no specific link to 2 John. And the title of "the elder" was widely used (1 Tim. 5:17, 19; Tit. 1:5; Jas 5:14; 1 Pet. 5:1, 5). Third John urges welcome for traveling "brothers" while 2 John urges much caution, even refusal, for traveling teachers.

First John shares some vocabulary with 2 and 3 John. But there are numerous differences among the writings. The "elder" who identifies himself as the author in both 2 and 3 John is absent from 1 John. The five chapters of 1 John and its doctrinal concerns construct a much longer document, a different genre and with quite different content. And 1 John does not seem to be interested in matters of "church" in the way that 3 John 9–10 does.

Again it seems we do not have enough information by which to reach a sustainable conclusion. Perhaps we could conclude that their authors are not the author of the Gospel of John, and that there are at least two, if not three, authors of the writings. All such imaginary authors probably align to varying degrees with a Johannine tradition. But that scenario involves considerable speculation without compelling support. We do not know who wrote them.

Likewise, the order of their composition is uncertain. Every possible configuration has been suggested: 1–2–3; 3–2–1; 2–3–1; 1–3–2. In addition to these numerous possibilities, the documents are undated. Some have suggested that the opponents condemned in 1 John largely fade in 2 John, which suggests 1 John is the first to be written followed by 2 John. But equally one could argue that 2 John comes first with just a passing reference to a situation that explodes in 1 John. What then to do with 3 John? Does it precede 2 and 1 John or follow 2 and 1 John?[3] And are the opponents actual figures or literary constructions useful for the arguments?

Finding a convincing way to address these questions has evaded interpreters. We simply cannot know the order in which these three documents were written.[4]

When Were 1, 2, and 3 John Written?

Given these various factors, it is not surprising that we cannot say with any precision when each of the writings was written. Yet we can at least suggest a general window in which they were composed.

---

[3]Discussion of these "opponents" or secessionists is extensive. Most commentaries include discussion of possible identifications. See John Painter, "The 'Opponents' in 1 John," *NTS* 32 (1986): 48–71; Daniel Streett, *They Went Out From Us: The Identity of the Opponents in First John.* BZNW 177 (Berlin: de Gruyter, 2011).

[4]I have discussed possible interactions among four documents commonly associated with a Johannine tradition: John's Gospel; 1, 2, and 3 John. Another New Testament document, the Book of Revelation, claims authorship by "John" (Rev. 1:1). We do not know who this John is. Because Revelation differs so significantly from these other four documents (its eschatological orientation; its retreat from the Roman empire which it declares to be in the control of the devil and under God's judgment), I do not discuss it. See Warren Carter, *What Does Revelation Reveal? Unlocking the Mystery* (Nashville: Abingdon, 2011).

One way of doing so is to identify writings that quote the Johannine documents. This would establish what is called a *terminus ad quem*, a time by which they had to be written. There is no clear citation from the writings until Irenaeus' citations (see pp. 7–8) from around 180 CE.

Are there any indications of an earlier date for the writings in the second century? There are several echoes that might suggest an earlier date. Bishop Polycarp of Smyrna, and, according to Irenaeus (*Adv. Her* 3.3), a disciple of John the Apostle, writes a letter to the Philippian believers around 140. In that letter, writing about deceiving false believers, Polycarp (7.1) states: "For everyone who does not confess Jesus Christ to have come in the flesh is antichrist." The declaration does not cite anything in the Johannine documents word for word, but it does draw together several important thoughts in them. The claim that those who fail to confess Jesus has come in the flesh are antichrists echoes similar statements in 2 Jn 7 as well as 1 Jn 4:2-3.

> . . . those who do not confess that Jesus Christ has come in the flesh; any such person is the deceiver and the antichrist
>
> (2 Jn 7)

> . . . every spirit that does not confess Jesus is not from God. And this is the spirit of the antichrist . . .
>
> (1 Jn 4:2-3)

Several other writings from around the 130s–140s—*Epistle of Barnabas; Shepherd of Barnabas*—might also employ some echoes of themes and language that are important in the Johannine writings.

These observations suggest that I and 2 John are known by around the 120s–130s. The references clarify neither the time nor the order of composition.

Third John is not included in these references. The first reference to 3 John comes a century later in the third century. Eusebius (*Hist. eccl.* 6.25.10) attributes to Origen a statement recognizing the existence of 2 and 3 John though "all do not consider them genuine," a reference that reflects doubts that John the apostle wrote them. Eusebius in the early fourth century locates 1 John with the clearly-recognized authoritative books for Jesus-communities, but lists 2 and 3 John among the "disputed books" even as he recognizes they are "well-known and acknowledged by most" (*Hist. eccl.* 3.24.17; 3.25.2-3).

Sometime before around 120s–130s, then, at least I and 2 John seem to be circulating. But we do not know their dating with any more precision. And the origins of 3 John remain elusive.

Where Were 1, 2, and 3 John Written?

The three documents give no indication of the location of their origin or recipients. Nor can we assume that the three writings address the same community. Further, were the writings addressed to specific communities or circulated among more general audiences? Or both? We do not know.

Scholars have suggested origins in the areas of Ephesus in Asia Minor, Antioch in Syria, and Alexandria in Egypt. Tradition has linked the Johannine traditions particularly to Ephesus and its surrounding area but there is no clear proof. We don't know where they were written.

To Whom Were They Written?

Discussion of the audiences for or recipients of each of the writings will emerge in the subsequent chapters. Here I note several general features.

- The recipients comprised people assumed to be Jesus-believers. The writings are neither evangelistic nor public.
- The writers ascribe authority to themselves and construct their addressees as subservient to them. The recipients are expected to comply with the writers' teachings and instructions. A character named Diotrephes is singled out in 3 John 9 for failing to recognize the writer's authority.
- Most of the recipients are anonymous. 1 John does not identify the "you" (plural) who are addressed, nor does 2 John name the "lady and her children." Only 3 John names Gaius as its addressee while also referring to Diotrephes and Demetrius.
- Groups of Jesus-believers met in houses or tenements. Groups were usually small in number. While often autonomous, they were also sometimes part of local networks with a leader.
- Based on studies of the Roman Empire and early Jesus-believers, the recipients are likely to be among non-elites of low socio-economic status. One analysis maps Roman society as a seven-tiered hierarchy comprising three tiers of elites, a middling order, and three tiers of non-elites or gradations of the poor. The poor made up some 70 or 80 percent of the population. They faced food insecurity, low immunity to

disease, hard manual work, and often short lifespans. Further, based on studies of the names of Jesus-believers in Romans 16, the addressees likely consisted of male and female, free, freed and slaves, and various ethnicities.[5]

Beyond these general features, we know few specifics about the writings' addressees.

Conclusion

In this chapter, I have discussed six aspects of these writings about which we have little definitive knowledge. I have suggested that we do not know for certain:

1   their authorship
2   their relationship to the Gospel of John and to each other
3   the order in which they were written
4   when they were written
5   where they were written; or 6) to whom they were written.

However, in the absence of definitive knowledge about these issues, interpreters have developed approaches to interpreting these writings. These approaches draw certain conclusions about these six questions, make some (reasonable) interpretive assumptions, and develop a framework for interpreting the writings. In the next two chapters, we will look at two such approaches, one that posits continuities across what we might call a Johannine tradition, the other emphasizing more the autonomy of each of the three writings.

---

[5]Steven Friesen, "Poverty in Pauline Studies: Beyond the So-Called New Consensus," *JSNT* 26 (2004): 322–61; Peter Lampe, "The Roman Church of Romans 16." In Karl P. Donfried (ed.), *The Romans Debate* (Grand Rapids: Baker Academic, 1977, 1991, 2005), 216–30.

2

Raymond Brown: Johannine Tradition and Community

In Chapter 1, I discussed six aspects of the Johannine writings about which we have no definitive knowledge. Yet in the absence of that knowledge, interpreters have nevertheless developed approaches and frameworks for interpreting these writings. These approaches draw certain conclusions about the issues discussed in Chapter 1, make some informed interpretive assumptions, and develop a framework for interpreting the writings.

In this chapter, we examine one such approach: Raymond Brown's very influential model.[1] This model—with some tweaking—has been the dominnt interpretive framework for these Johannine writings for much of the last fifty years.[2] In Chapter 3, we'll look at an alternative approach.

The Johannine Writings According to Raymond Brown

Brown recognizes that there are things we do not know about the Johannine community and these three writings. As he fills in gaps and makes interpretive decisions and assumptions, he admits that his reconstruction "claims at most probability." He expresses himself happy if readers find "sixty percent of my detective work [to be] accepted." Throughout his discussion he regularly

---

[1]I follow the discussion in Raymond Brown, *The Community of the Beloved Disciple: The Life, Loves, and Hates of an Individual Church in New Testament Times* (New York: Paulist Press, 1979), esp. 93–144. See also Brown, *The Epistles of John.* Anchor Bible 30 (Garden City: Doubleday, 1982). For a somewhat modified approach, Urban von Wahlde, *The Johannine Commandments: I John and the Struggle for the Johannine Tradition* (New York: Paulist, 1990).
[2]For example, John Painter, *1, 2, and 3 John* (Collegeville: Liturgical Press, 2002).

uses language such as "hypothesis" and "assume/assumption" as he makes his analysis.

With this caveat, Brown positions the three Johannine writings in a four-part sketch of a history of the Johannine Jesus-community that embraces John's Gospel and a couple of subsequent phases across the first and second centuries that include 1–3 John.

- Phase One: This pre-Gospel phase stretches from the mid-50s to the late 80s CE. This is the time of the origin of the Johannine community, expelled from a synagogue community after a time of conflict.

- Phase Two: During this phase, the Gospel of John is written around 90 CE. The expulsion from a synagogue has taken place but there is ongoing conflict and psychological scars. Some of the community affirmations about Jesus have alienated the Johannine community from a pluralistic world involving other Christian groups as well as non-believers who were largely unresponsive to the community's Gentile mission.

- Phase Three: This is the crucial time in Brown's scheme, the time of 1, 2, and 3 John around 100 CE. The Johannine community has experienced conflict and division (1 Jn 2:18-19). Brown's hypothesis is that some in the community misinterpreted four aspects of the Gospel: christology, ethics, eschatology, and pneumatology. These members left the community and seem to be attracting other members to join them (1 Jn 4:5). The writings, especially 1 and 2 John, address this situation and attempt to bolster the remaining members against these "secessionists."

- Phase Four: After the three writings were written, the now-divided Johannine community developed in two directions. Those who departed belong to groups known as Docetists, Gnostics, Cerinthians and Montanists (see Chapter 5 on opponents). Those who stayed merged into the developing church that will call itself orthodox or the "church catholic."

One of the aspects of Brown's model that has commended it to various interpreters is the way that it joins together the Gospel and the Johannine writings in a plausible historical trajectory. Our focus here will concentrate on his construction of Phase Three.

Absolutely central to his discussion of 1, 2, and 3 John is the division or schism that he sees attested in 1 John 2:18-19 and 2 John 7–8a.

Children, it is the last hour! As you have heard that antichrist is coming, so now many antichrists have come … They went out from us, but they did not belong to us; for if they had belonged to us, they would have remained with us. But by going out they made it plain that none of them belongs to us.

(1 Jn 2:18-19)

Many deceivers have gone out into the world, those who do not confess that Jesus Christ has come in the flesh; any such person is the deceiver and the antichrist! Be on your guard …

(2 Jn 7–8a)

Brown makes a series of interpretive decisions as he builds his model.

He "assumes" that all three documents are written by one author. He argues that the writings are locked together by overlapping themes. The same doctrinal and moral issues that derive from the schism occur in and draw together 1 and 2 John. Likewise, 2 and 3 John are linked by the concern with itinerant teachers. Brown concludes that this inter-linking reflects the work of one author. This author, though, is not the Beloved Disciple of John's Gospel. Brown posits a Johannine school of writers comprising at least an evangelist and a redactor responsible for the Gospel plus this author of the writings. This group faithfully transmits and interprets the tradition as witnesses to its truth.

Brown argues that John's Gospel is written before the writings and the writings are written in the canonical order of 1, 2, and 3 John. His main argument for this sequence is that the Gospel does not reflect the in-house division and conflict evident in 1 and 2 John. If the writings preceded the Gospel, the Gospel would reflect this struggle, which it does not do. Rather, he accounts for the conflict and division attested in 1 and 2 John as a result of debates over interpretations of the Gospel. The writings must, then, follow the Gospel, though 3 John does not fit very neatly.

Further, Brown suggests that what he calls the Johannine community comprises churches in different geographical locations. And, with small groups of Jesus-believers meeting in houses, perhaps there were several groups in the same town or city. First John, he surmises, addresses churches in a large metropolitan area like Ephesus, whereas 2 and 3 John are addressed to churches in other towns to which the author must travel (2 Jn 12; 3 Jn 14). He posits that the secessionists traveled to one of these scattered groups and threaten to divide it. That action necessitated the author to write 2 John to warn against those whom the author regards as false teachers. And, Brown "hypothesizes" that the author addresses another church's leader, Gaius, in another town in order to procure hospitality for the author's agents, including Demetrius, since Diotrephes was inhospitable to any visiting teachers (3 John). In positing these scenarios, Brown engages in considerable hypothesizing.

By far, Brown's discussion of 1, 2, and 3 John focuses on the schism or division that he posits as central to the community (communities?) that these documents address (1 Jn 2:19; 2 Jn 7). What happened? Who are these schismatics, secessionists, opponents? We have no account from the folks who have left.

Brown admits that his approach to this reconstruction is difficult. He recognizes that the only way of knowing about these folks is through a mirror-reading strategy. Brown makes the far-reaching "assumption" that 1 John is consistently polemical, that the author consistently attacks claims that these secessionists have made. He admits that "such a mirror-image approach has many perils." He concedes the possibility that the author might attack what he considers to be wrong ideas without our knowing if the opponents actually held them.

But having recognized these "perils," Brown proceeds with "a working hypothesis" that 1 John is fundamentally a polemical document in attacking those who have departed and their beliefs. And, he claims, the attacks reveal the "consistent body of thought" that these secessionists held.

Brown asks where these errant ideas originate. He surveys previous suggestions that these ideas come from outside groups (Gnostics; Docetists; Cerinthians) or groups that have recently joined the Johannine community (Gentiles; Hellenistic-Jewish philosophical folks; wandering charismatics). He dismisses these suggestions as "little more than guesses."

He argues his own "hypothesis" that at the heart of the dispute were arguments over interpretations of the Johannine tradition available in the Gospel of John. The disputes were not with outsiders who infiltrated the Jesus-community but were internal and in-house. They arose because members of the community disagreed over interpreting the Gospel. Brown identifies four areas in contention: christology, ethics, eschatology, and pneumatology. As far as the author of 1–2 John is concerned, the secessionists were not faithful interpreters of the tradition that the Gospel of John expresses. They distorted "what was from the beginning" (1 Jn 1:1). The dispute was beyond reconciliation and, according to the author, "they went out from us" (1 Jn 2:19).

Brown elaborates the four areas in dispute.

Christology

Brown claims these verses reflect the Christological matters in dispute:

> Who is the liar but the one who denies that Jesus is the Christ? This is the antichrist, the one who denies the Father and the Son.
>
> (1 Jn 2:22-23)

> And this is his commandment, that we should believe in the name of his Son Jesus Christ.
>
> (1 Jn 3:23)

> God abides in those who confess that Jesus is the Son of God, and they abide in God.
>
> (1 Jn 4:15)

> Everyone who believes that Jesus is the Christ has been born of God.
>
> (1 Jn 5:1)

> Who is it that conquers the world but the one who believes that Jesus is the Son of God?
>
> (I Jn 5:5)

He interprets these affirmations about the identity of Jesus with content provided by 1 Jn 4:2-3:

> every spirit that confesses that Jesus Christ has come in the flesh is from God, and every spirit that does not confess Jesus is not from God.

Brown focuses on the significance of the phrase "come in the flesh" as key to the argument over Jesus's identity.

> Many deceivers have gone out into the world, those who do not confess that Jesus Christ has come in the flesh;
>
> (2 Jn 7)

Brown reads these verses polemically as countering the secessionists' misinterpretations. He argues that they interpreted John's Gospel by emphasizing that as the pre-existent Word, who originates in heaven with God, Jesus made life available to humans. They did not deny Jesus's human existence but they did not view it as "salvifically significant." Jesus simply passed through this world; his life and death were of no consequence. Brown recognizes that parts of John's Gospel can lead to this interpretation but the author of 1 John regards it as an inadequate interpretation.

Against these erroneous claims the author confidently appeals to the reliable witness "from the beginning" about Jesus's human existence:

> what we have heard, what we have seen with our eyes, what we have looked at and touched with our hands, concerning the word of life—this life was revealed
>
> (1 Jn 1:1-2)

He affirms with repetition the importance of Jesus coming into the world as a human being to reveal God's love and life:

> God's love was revealed among us in this way: God sent his only Son into the world so that we might live through him . . . And we have seen and do testify that the Father has sent his Son as the Savior of the world.
>
> (1 Jn 4:9, 14)

> This is the one who came by water and blood, Jesus Christ.
>
> (1 Jn 5:6)

In addition to Jesus revealing God's love and life in his activity, Jesus's death takes away sins:

> and the blood of Jesus his Son cleanses us from all sin . . . But if anyone does sin, we have an advocate with the Father, Jesus Christ the righteous; and he is the atoning sacrifice for our sins, and not for ours only but also for the sins of the whole world.
>
> (1 Jn 1:7; 2:2)

> You know that he was revealed to take away sins.
>
> (1 Jn 3:5)

> We know love by this, that he laid down his life for us.
>
> (1 Jn 3:16)

> In this is love, not that we loved God but that he loved us and sent his Son to be the atoning sacrifice for our sins.
>
> (1 Jn 4:10)

Against the secessionists' minimal attention to the significance of Jesus's human existence (as Brown reconstructs them), Brown sees the author of 1 John affirming that Jesus's identity as Christ and Son of God encompasses his activity among humans in revealing God's love and life. Furthermore, his death—with its salvific significance—takes away sins.

Ethics

Brown argues that the divisive or schismatic dispute also involves ethical implications from the Christological disagreements. Reading "in mirror fashion," Brown argues that the secessionists made three claims.

The first asserts that their intimacy with God means they are sinless and perfect. Brown points out that some of the statements in John's Gospel could lead to this claim. The Gospel constructs Jesus-believers as walking or living in light not darkness (John 8:12). While non-believers remain in sin as slaves of sin (John 8:24; 9:41), Jesus has set believers free (8:31-34).

Brown reads 1 John 1:8, 10 as the secessionists' claims: "we have no sin … we have not sinned" (1 Jn 1:8, 10). The writer of 1–2 John rejects the claim:

> If we say that we have no sin, we deceive ourselves, and the truth is not in us.
>
> (1 Jn 1:8)

> If we say that we have not sinned, we make him a liar, and his word is not in us.
>
> (1 Jn 1:10)

Jesus's death provides forgiveness for confessed sin (1 Jn 1:9). Yet, as Brown points out, there is a somewhat challenging passage in 1 John 3 in which it seems that the author comes very close to agreeing with the secessionists:

> No one who abides in him sins; no one who sins has either seen him or known him. … Everyone who commits sin is a child of the devil … Those who have been born of God do not sin, because God's seed abides in them; they cannot sin, because they have been born of God.
>
> (1 Jn 3:6-9 selections)

What's the difference between what Brown sees 1 John as rejecting in 1 John 1:8-10, and what this passage in 1 John 3 advocates?

Brown argues that the author of 1 John recognizes that sinlessness is the obligation or goal but not yet the accomplished reality that the secessionists claim. Brown suggests that the writer opposes a life of sinfulness; a follower of Jesus "cannot *consistently* be a sinner." Brown points to 1 John 2:1-2:

> My little children, I am writing these things to you so that you may not sin. But if anyone does sin, we have an advocate with the Father, Jesus Christ the righteous; and he is the atoning sacrifice for our sins.

We should note that 1 John does not use the adverb "consistently."

Brown identifies a second ethical claim that he thinks the secessionists make, namely that their behavior has no salvific importance. Just as they claimed Jesus's earthly life and death had no significance, nor do their lives have any significance for salvation. They do not care about the commandments. Again Brown posits that this view is an erroneous interpretation of Gospel passages such as: "You do not belong to the world for I chose you out of the world" (John 15:19; 17:16).

> Brown identifies the letter writer responding in two ways. One is a direct approach.
>
> Now by this we may be sure that we know him, if we obey his commandments. Whoever says, "I have come to know him," but does not obey his commandments, is a liar.
>
> (1 Jn 2:3-4)
>
> All who obey his commandments abide in him, and he abides in them.
>
> (1 Jn 3:24)

The letter writer's second approach attacks the link they make with Jesus. Instead of arguing that "just as" there is no significance to Jesus's earthly existence, the author urges righteous lives "just as" Christ lived.

> Whoever says, "I abide in him," ought to walk just as he walked.
>
> (1 Jn 2:6)
>
> And all who have this hope in him purify themselves, just as he is pure.
>
> (1 Jn 3:3)
>
> Everyone who does what is right is righteous, just as he is righteous.
>
> (1 Jn 3:7)

Brown admits that the writer at this point "is noticeably vague on details" of Jesus's life.

Brown identifies a third ethical issue, namely the secessionists' failure to love the brothers and sisters of the community. Such love is commanded in John's Gospel (13:34-35; 15:12). Brown interprets the secessionists' departure as showing a lack of love that breaks relationships, a hatred for community members, and thus accounts for the writing's emphasis on love:

> And this is his commandment, that we should . . . love one another, just as he has commanded us.
>
> (1 Jn 3:23)
>
> But whoever hates another believer is in the darkness, walks in the darkness.
>
> (1 Jn 2:11)
>
> Those who say, "I love God," and hate their brothers or sisters, are liars; for those who do not love a brother or sister whom they have seen, cannot love

God whom they have not seen. The commandment we have from him is this: those who love God must love their brothers and sisters also.

(1 Jn 4:20-21)

Ironically, this intra-communal love does not mean reaching out and welcoming opponents. Second John is very suspicious of visitors to the Jesus communities and warns against welcoming them.

Do not receive into the house or welcome anyone who comes to you and does not bring this teaching; for to welcome is to participate in the evil deeds of such a person.

(2 Jn 10–11)

Brown comments that the author provides justification for "hating other Christians for the love of God."

According to Brown, the secessionists make three erroneous interpretations of John's Gospel to claim sinlessness; to neglect ethical living (in imitation of Jesus); and to hate community members rather than love them. These three ethical issues are part of the intra-communal conflicts and schism.

Eschatology

Brown admits "there are no clear eschatological statements that the author condemns." Nevertheless, Brown presses on to assert that the opponents' claims to perfection and sinlessness express a realized eschatology. This realized eschatology is consonant with Gospel emphases such as no future judgment (John 3:18-19; 5:24) and the experience of eternal life now (5:24; 6:54; 11:26). And the author of 1 John shares similar affirmations of present eschatology: the evil one is conquered (1 Jn 2:13-14); eternal life or life of the age is revealed now (1 Jn 1:2); believers are God's children (1 Jn 3:1).

Yet the author corrects the opponents' affirmations in two ways. One is that he links present eschatology to ethical living. Doing justice and loving brothers and sisters are marks of being God's children now (1 Jn 3:10).

And the author qualifies present eschatology with elements of future eschatology. He polemicizes the secessionists' false claim of a fully realized eschatology. More is to be revealed and ethical living in the present is required to participate in it:

Beloved, we are God's children now; what we will be has not yet been revealed. What we do know is this: when he is revealed, we will be like him, for we will see him as he is. And all who have this hope in him purify themselves, just as he is pure.

(1 Jn 3:2-3)

And now, little children, abide in him, so that when he is revealed we may have confidence and not be put to shame before him at his coming.

(1 Jn 2:28)

And the author declares that the existence of the opponents (antichrists and false prophets) signals the imminent end of the age:

Children, it is the last hour! As you have heard that antichrist is coming, so now many antichrists have come. From this we know that it is the last hour.

(1 Jn 2:18)

Brown argues that the author polemicizes against the secessionists' exclusively realized eschatology by linking it to ethical requirements for present living and by emphasizing that present living leads to accountability in a future eschatology.

Pneumatology

Brown begins by citing 1 John 4:1-2:

Beloved, do not believe every spirit, but test the spirits to see whether they are from God; for many false prophets have gone out into the world. By this you know the Spirit of God: every spirit that confesses that Jesus Christ has come in the flesh is from God

From this exhortation, Brown posits that the secessionists claimed the Spirit's sanction for their claims and teaching. They could appeal to the Gospel's teaching about the spirit or Paraclete who continues Jesus's presence among them forever (John 14:16) and who teaches believers everything (John 14:26), bears witness to Jesus (15:26), and guides them into all truth (16:13).

The writer of 1 John does not dispute the Spirit's presence. Rather, he insists on testing the Spirits to discern if it is the Spirit of God and truth or the spirit of antichrist and error. The true Spirit testifies to Jesus.

By this you know the Spirit of God: every spirit that confesses that Jesus Christ has come in the flesh is from God, and every spirit that does not confess Jesus is not from God. And this is the spirit of the antichrist . . . We are from God. Whoever knows God listens to us, and whoever is not from God does not listen to us. From this we know the spirit of truth and the spirit of error.

(1 Jn 4:2-6)

The test is doctrinal; the true Spirit from God testifies that Jesus has come in the flesh. And it is social in that those who make this confession belong to the community of those aligned with the author. The writer declares that "you have been anointed by the Holy One" (1 Jn 2:20). This "anointing . . . abides in you, and so you do not need anyone to teach you" (1 Jn 2:27).

Brown acknowledges that this test and the assurances of the Spirit's teaching were "ineffectual." The teaching of the opponents and the subsequent division demonstrate its ineffectiveness.

Conclusion

Brown's approach is a mirror-reading of 1, 2, and 3 John. He locates these writings in Phase Three of a four-phase history of the Johannine tradition and community. He argues that the writings, from around 100 CE, are grounded in an intra-communal conflict and division. Some in the community have mis-interpreted aspects of the Gospel of John in four areas: christology, ethics, eschatology, and pneumatology. These members have created a schism and left the community. They seem to be attracting a significant number of other members to join them (1 Jn 4:5). For Brown, 1 and 2 John polemicize against the misinterpretations of the secessionists, and attempt to bolster the remaining members against these "secessionists" by setting forth the true interpretation of John's Gospel.

Evaluation

Brown's comprehensive reconstruction has, with a few modifications from sympathetic allies, dominated interpretations of 1–3 John over the last fifty years. Its construction of four phases of a Johannine community, its aligning of the Johannine Gospel and the three writings, its foregrounding of the schism, its internal "logic" of identifying misinterpretations of John's Gospel as the root of the schism, and his identification of four inter-related areas of debate repelled by 1 and 2 John in offering the "true" interpretations have provided a compelling analysis. It is a remarkable accomplishment.

Yet it is not without its problems.

Brown's method of mirror-reading is, as Brown recognizes, perilous. He declares himself to be happy if we readers accept 60 percent of his analysis. But he does not specify which 60 percent might be acceptable and which forty percent might not be. How do we know the difference? His interpretations rest on various assumptions that cannot be verified with any certainty.

For example, he chooses to place 1 John 2:18-19 at the center of his whole analysis, thereby centering the schism. Such a decision is questionable at best when the schism is explicitly referenced only there and at 2 John 7, and these verses can be interpreted very differently. It can be argued that some sort of separation has taken place but is it central to the three writings; if it *is* central or important, important for whom? Why does it receive so little direct attention?

And exactly what has happened? Brown pays little attention to the wording of 1 John 2:18 that mentions the departure of some. It reads, "As you have heard," and not "as you have experienced." This wording suggests that the recipients of 1 John did not experience the schism, as Brown assumes. They have heard about it but it does not seem to be central to their experience. And verse 18 goes on to say that these people have gone out "from us," with the "us" being the writers. They did not go out "from you," the recipients of the writing. These considerations suggest 1 John 2:18 is a report to the recipients of 1 John about something that they did not experience. This careful reading casts considerable doubt on Brown's construction that the recipients of 1 John have lived through a traumatic and all-defining division and that 1 John attacks these opponents or secessionists who have inflicted great harm on them.

Consistent with his reconstruction, Brown chooses to read 1–2 John as polemics against these schismatic opponents. Any and every affirmation in the writings is made, he posits, because the writer is attacking claims that the opponents/secessionists were making. By this means he identifies the four disputed categories of Christology, ethics, eschatology, and pneumatology. Yet how does Brown know to read these writings as polemics? How does he know, for example, that when 1 John counters a claim that some do not sin (1 Jn 1:8, 10), it must be a claim made by the secessionists?

And consistent with these decisions, Brown chooses to position John's Gospel before the three writings and to see the dispute and division as a matter of different interpretations of the Gospel.

Yet the fit is not always perfect. Brown recognizes there could be multiple Jesus groups in the main center of the tradition—perhaps Ephesus. But it is not clear how he imagines the schism. Did all of these groups experience the same split in the same way with the same secessionists? And did the other communities he posits in outlying areas also experience the schism?

If the Christological dispute is about the salvific significance or otherwise of Jesus's life, why do the writings not rehearse some of the Gospel's accounts of his earthly activity, like healings, feedings, conflicts, callings, and teachings? The Gospel offers plenty of material to refute such a claim beyond references to Jesus's death yet 1 John does not do so. And more fundamentally, why should the phrase "come in the flesh" be interpreted as refuting a claim that Jesus's life has no salvific value? That interpretation is not particularly compelling. If 1 John's emphasis on coming in the flesh is polemical, it would seem more likely that it resists opponents claiming Jesus had no earthly existence. But since that claim would be so at odds with the whole Gospel (1 Jn:14), it would be impossible to argue that the "opponents" had somehow misinterpreted the Gospel to reach this conclusion! This challenge in turn raises questions about Brown's insistence that the writings are to be read in relation to the Gospel.

In order to argue that the opponents interpret the Gospel to claim that ethical living is of no significance, Brown must overlook numerous Gospel passages that clearly identify ethical living and its salvific-eschatological significance. In addition to the love commandment, the Gospel commends service (John 13:14), feeding hungry people (6:1-14), and healing sick people (4:46-54; 5:1-18) thereby imitating Jesus's works (14:12). It also identifies various unethical behaviors such as "evil deeds" (3:19), murder (John 7:19; 8:37, 40), lying (8:44), stealing (10:1, 10; 12:6), and terrorist attacks against property and personnel (10:8). And the Gospel gives ethical living salvific and eschatological significance; doing good or doing evil determines one's fate in the resurrection (5:29). That's a lot of content to ignore in order to make a claim that the Gospel is being misinterpreted in relation to its ethical content.

Brown admits difficulties in identifying any eschatological statements from the opponents and has to extrapolate eschatological significance from claims of sinlessness, not an obvious source.

And 2 and 3 John figure little in his analysis. Brown's Johannine letters are largely reduced to just one non-letter, 1 John.

More foundational issues will emerge in the next chapter. Not surprisingly, some recent interpreters have rejected some of Brown's assumptions and starting points. For example, some have decentered the schism and the opponents or secessionists as the focus for interpreting the writings. Some have chosen not to foreground mirror-readings. Some have chosen not to read the writings as polemical but rather as identity-securing, pastorally oriented writings for community members. Perhaps the writings are more affirmations for those in the communities than polemic against opponents. And perhaps each of the writings should be engaged on its own terms, rather than as derivative from John's Gospel, located in a linear tradition, and consumed by a schism.

In the next chapter, we take a second run at these writings by considering a different interpretation that pursues these alternative approaches.

3

Judith Lieu's Approach: Three Autonomous Writings

A number of interpreters of 1–3 John have developed approaches to interpreting these writings that differ significantly from the widely embraced model of Raymond Brown discussed in Chapter 2. They have questioned central aspects of that model for making meaning of these writings. In this chapter, I feature the work of Judith Lieu as representative of an alternative way of making meaning of 1, 2, and 3 John.

In a series of studies, Lieu has constructed a very different picture of 1–3 John. She describes this picture as "diametrically opposed . . . in multiple ways" to the "approach based on the 'history of the community of the Beloved Disciple.'"[1] This last phrase, of course, refers to Brown's method. Lieu, on the other hand:

- rejects the approach that seeks to recover a history of the Johannine documents and of the/a Johannine community/communities. She does not think this history can be recovered. And she is agnostic as to whether there even was such a community.
- She does not foreground a Johannine tradition with recognizable central figures as authorities who produce the writings. No factors associate these writings with John the son of Zebedee, the Beloved Disciple.
- She respects the relative anonymity of the writings' authors and audiences.

---

[1] Judith Lieu, "The Audience of the Johannine Letters." In R. Alan Culpepper and Paul N. Anderson (eds), *Communities in Dispute: Current Scholarship on the Johannine Epistles* (Atlanta: SBL, 2014), 123–40. Also, Terry Griffith, "A Non-Polemical Reading of 1 John: Sin, Christology, and the Limits of Johannine Christianity," *Tyndale Bulletin* 49.2 (1998): 253–76.

- She does not argue for identifiable opponents and does not make the purported schism of 1 John 2:18-19 central to her interpretation of 1 and 2 John.
- She does not assume a fixed community across the three writings.
- She does not argue for a particular time and place of origin for the writings.

Despite these significant departures from Brown's approach, Lieu and Brown's methods share a common feature. Both approaches are committed to producing a construct of the Johannine writings and "communities." Both scholars use their imaginations and interpretive skills to make meaning of these writings. What meanings, then, does Lieu formulate?

Lieu's Construction and Method

Lieu notes that 1–3 John do not offer any information about their location, neither their place of origin or their destination. Nor does she find convincing evidence that they exist in literary dependence on the Gospel and each other. She acknowledges that 3 John does name Gaius, Diotrephes, and Demetrius as part of a Johannine community tradition, but questions whether they can be identified as prominent in any specific "Johannine" context. Lieu recognizes that the writings share a family likeness constituted by a dualistic worldview, common vocabulary, patterns of argument, and ideas. These features, in Lieu's view, attest neither common authorship nor literary dependence since these features can be imitated readily.[2] Rather, they indicate a tradition from which the writings draw in places.

These observations serve to reduce and reframe three aspects of Brown's construction, namely a clearly identified Johannine community, an identifiable determinative tradition, and, identifiable esteemed leaders and authors. Lieu does recognize some intertextuality between, for example, the Gospel of John and 1 John, but does not think this points to recoverable literary dependence. Lieu's alternative approach is to interpret each writing "on their own" and "without reference to the Gospel" rather than to an authoritative individual as author, while recognizing some aspects of a family likeness (vocabulary, dualism). On this basis she seeks to interpret each of the writings.

---

[2]Judith Lieu, *I, II, & 3 John: A Commentary* (Louisville: Westminster John Knox, 2008), 4.

1 John

This writing offers no names or location for its sender/author and recipients. Nor does it provide any back story that links author and recipients. It also lacks features of a letter—no greeting, health wish, thanksgiving, final greetings. Yet the writing addresses its audience directly with the second person plural pronoun "you." There are no differentiations or subgroups within this "you." The writing seeks "fellowship" between "we/us" and the audience "you" (1 Jn 1:3). Along with the first person plural pronoun "we" (1 Jn 1:6-10), the writer uses the first-person singular ("I write," 13x) to express the writing's purpose (1 Jn 2:1, 7, 8, 12-14, 21; 5:13). The writing thus functions as a letter to address its audience and situation, even as significant features of the genre of a letter are missing.

The author seeks "fellowship" with the audience (1 Jn 1:3). The writing elaborates the nature and basis of this privileged fellowship: it is "with the Father and the son" (1 Jn 1:3); it locates "God's children" apart from "the world" that is under the power of the evil one (1 Jn 5:19); it is marked by a dualistic world view of insiders and outsiders throughout (1 Jn 4:4-6).

The writer addresses the recipients as "my little children" and "children" (1 Jn 2:1, 18) thereby asserting his (?) superior and authoritative position but without providing a basis for it. In fact, the author reveals almost nothing about himself. The personal "I" signifies his authorship (1 Jn 2:1, 7 etc.) yet the plural "we" links him to a larger group (how big?) without elaborating the relationship. It is unclear as to whether there is any relationship between this author and the Elder/s of 2 and 3 John.

First John constructs a threefold past for the recipients. First is the activity of the Son, which initially is not related to the audience ("you") but only to "us," the authors (1 Jn 2:1-2; 4:9-10). This activity is named in the Prologue of 1 John 1:1-2 as concerning what "we" heard, saw, and touched. Just what this review refers to is not clear.

But then, second, "you," members of the audience, seem only now to be hearing the writing's proclamation (1 Jn 1:2, 3, 5). Yet the writing indicates that "you" have heard it in the past. The authors ("we") recognize that the recipients can share in fellowship with the Father and Son (1 Jn 1:3, 5), and acknowledge that they have already heard from the beginning, had sin forgiven, and conquered (1 Jn 2:7, 12-14, 18, 20-1, 24).

And third, in the past the unspecified "we" have experienced the going out of "antichrists" (1 Jn 2:18-19). Lieu's construction here of the so-called schism and opponents significantly differs from the commonly received picture that Brown constructed. She does not make this event central to her interpretation of 1 John. She points out that this "going out" was not something that the addressees experienced. "You" have *heard* about it (1 Jn 2:18) but did not experience it. It happened to the authorial "us" (4x, 1 Jn 2:19); "they went out from us," not the addressees. It is not, then, a central and traumatic event in the audience's past that impacts its present as many interpretations such as Brown's analysis claim. Lieu emphasizes that this differentiation between the experience of "us/we" and "you" has often been ignored in reconstructions of the writing's audience.

First John also constructs a significant future. One element is the return of Jesus which is to be greeted with confidence and boldness without fear (1 Jn 2:28; 3:21). Both "we" and "you," the "little children" and "children of God," await this return. Second, in the meantime, the audience is to abide, not be deceived, and to exhibit right belief and love. All of this the audience already knows (1 Jn 2:21, 26).

> I write to you not because you do not know the truth but because you know it . . . I write these things to you concerning those who would deceive you . . . As for you the anointing you have received from him abides in you and so you do not need anyone to teach you . . .

Lieu recognizes that in Chapters 1–3, the interplay of "we" and "you" has fluctuated. On one hand is the authorial "we" that is distinct from "you" the audience. Yet in other instances, "we" includes both author/s and audience: "he is the means of forgiveness for *our* sins" (1 Jn 2:2, emphasis added). In 1 John 4:4, the writers recognize "you are from God," and then declare in 4:6, that "we are from God." The "we" exist over against the "false prophets (who) have gone into the world" (1 Jn 4:1). The "world listens to them" (1 Jn 4:5), but "whoever knows God listens to us and whoever is not from God does not listen to us" (1 Jn 4:6). The "fellowship" that the authors seek with the audience in the opening verses is now accomplished (1 Jn 1:3, 6-7).

Moreover, Lieu notes that the conceptual world that the writing constructs is marked by dualisms such as light and darkness, love and hatred, the world in contrast to what is of God, being children of God or of the devil. This world is closed and coherent—almost, because the writing recognizes the possibility of insiders sinning (1 Jn 3:4-10; 1 Jn 1:8–2:2). To not believe, abide, or love means to exclude oneself from the children of God. And there is no place for dialogue with or mission amongst the world. The future requires "abiding" until the certain appearing of Jesus when "we will be like him" (1 Jn 3:2).

In the writer's dualism are outsiders such as "antichrists" (1 Jn 2:18). They are defined by "going out," by rejecting "us" (the writers), and by denying "the

Father and the Son" (1 Jn 2:19-22). They belong to the world (1 Jn 4:1, 5) that listens to them but not to us (1 Jn 4:5-6). They fail to be true.

The level of threat from these antichrists and false prophets seems somewhat indistinct. Indeed there are "false prophets" whose spirits need testing (1 Jn 4:1) and the spirit of antichrist is already in the world (1 Jn 4:3). The existence of these figures has eschatological significance for the writer. It indicates that the end of this age is near: "it is the last hour" (1 Jn 2:18). Presumably they will face condemnation while the recipients are divinely vindicated. Their identity, however, is elusive.

Yet the writer gives them little press. His audience has heard of "many antichrists" who departed from the authorial "us" though not from "you," the audience. Their departure revealed their false identity (1 Jn 2:18-19). The dispute seems to involve Christological confessions. They deny, according to the writer, that "Jesus is the Christ" (1 Jn 2:22; 5:1) and that "Jesus Christ has come in the flesh" (1 Jn 4:2). But the writer does not present them as posing immediate danger to the audience because the audience "has been anointed by the Holy One" and they "know the truth" (1 Jn 2:20-1). Their defense is to abide in what they know (1 Jn 2:26-8), to live on the right side of the dualistic worldview that the writing constructs.

In Lieu's analysis, 1 John is much more concerned with securing the faithfulness of the recipients than dwelling on those outside this audience. The writing does not urge any ecclesial discipline or action against those who "went out from us." It does recognize vindication in the judgment for the faithful audience (1 Jn 4:17) which implies condemnation for the unfaithful. Throughout, the writing's dualistic world view—the children of God versus the children of the devil (1 Jn 3:8-10), "us" against "the world" (1 Jn 2:15-17; 3:1; 4:5-7) – shapes the identity of the audience. These indistinct opponents provide a foil or contrast for naming the characteristics that should mark the identity and lifestyle of the writing's audience.

2 John

Lieu acknowledges that 2 John is a very different writing, a letter, with interaction between the writer and addressee, the elder and the "lady." Its central concern focuses on recognizing itinerant false teachers and deceivers. The author/elder warns the recipients to be watchful and not receive them (2 Jn 7–11).

Compared with 3 John, 2 John has a longer but stereotypical greeting (2 Jn 1–3) yet similar conclusion (2 Jn 12–13). The author addresses an audience which comprises a woman, her family (2 Jn 1), and wider community (2 Jn 7–12). The identity of the woman is not clear. The final verse indicates she has a sister with children (2 Jn 13). Lieu suggests there is elision between the idea of an individual and of a group that is configured in some way through the individual. Nor is her role specified, though some interpreters who consider her to be a real person have understood her to be the community's leader.

The author names himself "the Elder." Is this the same author as 3 John or another "elder"? There's a more basic question that Lieu raises. Is this "Elder" (and the Lady for that matter) a real person in a real situation or are they both fictional constructs in the narrative fiction that serve the purpose of conveying instructions about not receiving false teachers? Letters can employ anonymity or pseudonymity (evoking an authoritative foundational figure as in 1–2 Pet. and 1–2 Tim.) to offer instruction.

Whereas in 3 John the elder refers to "my children" (3 Jn 4), the children in 2 John remain "your children," the woman's children (2 Jn 4, 13). Both letters open with an expression of love (2 Jn 1; 3 Jn 1) though the woman is not addressed as "beloved" as Gaius is in 3 John. Whereas in 3 John, the author uses the vocative to address Gaius three times (3 Jn 2, 5, 11), 2 John addresses the woman with the vocative only once (2 Jn 5). The relationship between the Elder and the elect lady seems more distant and less personal than that of the Elder and Gaius.

After this initial address, the letter expands its audience. Verses 1-5a address the woman in the singular and joyfully celebrate the faithfulness of her household (2 Jn 4). Verses 5b-6a move to the plural in aligning the author and the lady in the command that we "love one another" and "walk according to his commandments." Thereafter the second person plural addresses the audience until verse 12 with two ethical commands: beware of deceivers and antichrists (2 Jn 8–9) and do not welcome false teachers into "the house" (2 Jn 10–11). The author claims authority in instructing the group how to behave vis-à-vis not receiving false teachers and deceivers. This emphasis differs from the exhortations in 3 John to receive itinerant figures. Verse 13 returns to the singular in the final greetings for the lady.

The warning about not receiving itinerant false teachers is contained within expectations about the coming of Jesus and his reward (2 Jn 8). The elder gravely warns about the threat posed by these "many deceivers" and "antichrist" who have gone out into the world (2 Jn 7). He instructs against receiving one ("him") who might threaten to enter "the house" and who represents "evil deeds" (2 Jn 10). Their destructive impact involves both "losing what we have worked for" and participating in their evil (2 Jn 8, 11). These figures offer false Christological teaching ("Jesus Christ has [not] come in the flesh") and does not "abide in the teaching of Christ" (2 Jn 7–10). Lieu notes that 2 Jn 7 redirects the confession of 1 John 4:2-3 in replacing the latter's perfect tense with a present participle, thereby reducing the emphasis on a specific time and mode of coming, and employing a familiar Johannine epithet for Jesus. The elder names their errant confession though the precise content of the unacceptable confession is not elaborated. These concerns provide the criteria by which to discern the false or true teacher. The letter constructs conflicting teachers and styles of leadership: a vulnerable local leader of the group in her house, a leader perhaps of a small network (the elder) who is concerned for the faithfulness of the recipients of the letter, and itinerant teachers who bring false teaching.

By contrast with such damaging arrivals is the future joyful coming of the elder himself (2 Jn 12).

Lieu's discussion of the letter's genre, the possible fictional characterization of the Elder and the lady, their interactions and relationship, their anonymous and unspecified identities, the letter's narrative of past and desired future actions, and its recognition of possible conflict and contested authority, highlight likely contours of the situation in which the letter participates and which it constructs. A recognition of these factors undermines a method of interpreting the writing that assumes common "Johannine" authors, well-connected "Johannine" communities, and/or in interactions with other "Johannine" writings.

3 John

Lieu identifies 3 John as a personal letter between the unnamed writer, the Elder, and his addressee, Gaius. It resembles the private letters written on papyrus that have been found in the rubbish dumps of ancient Egypt. Its brevity is probably determined by the length of a papyrus sheet.

The personal nature of the communication between the Elder and Gaius is evident in several ways. One means involves the singular forms of address that mark the letter. The writer addresses Gaius with the endearment, "beloved" (3 Jn 1, 2, 5, 11), four times in the singular. The second person pronoun "you" and singular vocative address occur twelve times in fifteen verses, and the first-person singular verb forms (I) occur eleven times. These forms of expression thereby heighten the sense of a personal, relational interaction. In the final greetings of verses 13-15, the "I" (the Elder) and singular "you" language (Gaius) emphasize this personal address and relationship between the two.

Others are involved in the relationship between the elder and Gaius. The Elder refers to "friends/brothers and sisters" in verses 5 and 10 who have visited Gaius and reported to their church in verse 9. The defiant Diotrephes and mysterious Demetrius appear briefly, the former in resistant relation to the writer (3 Jn 9–10), the later as a model for Gaius (3 Jn 11–12). The focus therefore remains on the relationship between the Elder and Gaius.

Gaius seems to be a leader of a house-community. Yet he is not so identified, though references to "the church" in 3 John 9–10 suggest such leadership. Nevertheless, Gaius is the writing's main audience.

The Elder's role is not identified either. He could be a leader of churches in an area, or a supervisor for Gaius and other church leaders, but nothing is elaborated (3 Jn 5–6).

Lieu wonders whether the named persons are historical persons or narrative fictions. As with 2 John, she notes that anonymous and pseudonymous writings were common in early Christian letters. The use of the conventions of narrative fictions would frame a letter for a generalized audience with the named figures representative of a situation involving extending hospitality to itinerant teachers.

Lieu pursues her argument that 3 John should be considered on its own terms by identifying the particular narrative involving the past, present, and future that it constructs.

She describes the narrative of 3 John as episodic, not linear. Its content largely concerns the past. Unidentified itinerant brothers and sisters/friends had visited the elder. Their arrival suggests some sort of "network," though the nature, structure, and members of this "network" remain elusive (3 Jn 3). The Elder recognizes that Gaius welcomed them with hospitality and they subsequently departed to make a good report to an unspecified "church" (3 Jn 5–6). The Elder had written to Diotrephes but he rejected the Elder's letter and the itinerant brothers or "friends" who had been sent to him (3 Jn 9–10). The identity of Diotrephes is not clear but *if* the Elder oversees churches in an area and *if* Gaius is a church leader, it is likely Diotrephes is also. His rejection of the Elder's agents suggests an unelaborated conflict and contesting of the Elder's claim to issue directives. The Elder constructs Diotrephes as not only rejecting the Elder's authority but as self-promoting, as badmouthing the Elder, as not welcoming the agents, and expelling those who did want to welcome them from the church (3 Jn 9–10).

Utilizing the contrast or rhetorical technique of *synkrisis*, the Elder exhorts Gaius to continue to extend the hospitality that the undefined Demetrius provides (3 Jn 11–12). This exhortation to welcome itinerants is the purpose of the narrative. At some future point the Elder might visit and, it is implied, expects to be welcomed with hospitality (3 Jn 10).

To accomplish this purpose of exhortation, 3 John's strategy is to create "presence" and relationship. In the opening eight verses Gaius is constructed as autonomous. The elder recognizes and commends his treatment of the itinerant brothers and sisters. In verses 9-12, the Elder seeks to ally Gaius with himself as he encourages his continuing welcoming action. He is not to imitate Diotrephes because Diotrephes does not recognize the Elder's authority. Rather he is to ally with Demetrius, who seems to have done the good thing and welcomed the agents. The contrast of the actions of the two figures exemplifies the right behavior that the author seeks from Gaius (and any other readers). To not welcome itinerants supported by the Elder would be to reject the Elder and his authority.

The writer of 3 John, then, seeks to secure Gaius' loyalty in a context of a threat to the author's position and authority. The challenge comes from Diotrephes who "likes to put himself first" and "does not acknowledge our authority" (3 Jn 9). He also "spreads false charges against us," refuses to welcome the brothers and sisters, and expels from the church those who want to welcome the brothers and sisters (3 Jn 10).

At the center of these five-fold charges, as the writer presents it, is not a doctrinal dispute but a practice concerning authority. Diotrephes does not acknowledge the author's/Elder's authority as expressed in a letter the author had written "to the church" (3 Jn 9). The content of that letter is not rehearsed; perhaps it was a letter of commendation for the itinerants that should have ensured their welcome. In their rejection the writer finds a rejection of himself, along with (unspecified) slander against him. Diotrephes exerts his own authority over "the church" in expelling those who align themselves with the writer's practice of welcome. The Elder writes to secure the beloved Gaius' allegiance, renouncing Diotrephes' inhospitable and excluding "evil," and practicing welcome for those who are "co-workers with the truth" and who come "from God," like Demetrius (3 Jn 8, 11-12).

Lieu points to the well-known problem for Jesus-groups of recognizing "true" itinerant and/or charismatic teachers who visit local groups. The letter indicates conflict not only over the receiving of these brothers and sisters but also over how decisions are made about their reception and by whom. Details are scarce. Perhaps the Elder (as an area overseer?) endorsed them,

Gaius received them (perhaps for his church?), Diotrephes did not (perhaps for his church?), and Demetrius did so (perhaps for his church?). Perhaps the conflict involves local, autonomous leaders (Gaius? Diotrephes? Demetrius?) and area leaders like the Elder who claimed some leadership and authority over a network of some local communities and who seeks to secure Gaius' allegiance in the face of Diotrephes' defiant independence. Whatever the specific contours of the parties involved, tensions or struggles over leadership styles and sources of sanction, as well as of recognizing legitimate itinerants, seem important.

Lieu's discussion of the writing's genre as a letter, the personal relationship between the Elder and Gaius, their anonymous and unspecified identities, its narrative of past and desired future actions, its strategy of emphasizing presence and relationship, and its recognition of conflict and contested authority, undermines a method that locates the writing in the context of well-connected Johannine communities. One feature of the letter is its significant lack of typical Johannine vocabulary. It uses non-Johannine language such as "church" (3 Jn 6, 9) and the verbs "send them on" (3 Jn 6), "puts himself first," "not acknowledge/welcome," and "talk nonsense/spread false charges" (3 Jn 9–10). By emphasizing the individuality of this writing, she argues against the method of using assumptions about the collection of Johannine writings and a Johannine tradition as the starting point to interpreting it.

Conclusion

Lieu's approach is to not use the purported "Johannine character or tradition" of the writings to prejudge their interpretation. She acknowledges signs of their interrelationships such as similar closings of 2 and 3 John, the antichrists of 1 and 2 John who do not confess Jesus has come in the flesh, and some common vocabulary. She recognizes, though, that interpreters have often appealed to a Johannine tradition to "fill the vacuum" of unknowns in the Johannine writings, and that it provides resonance for the antithesis of those "from God" and those who do evil who have not seen God (3 Jn 11; John 8:47). The Gospel and 1 John share some common language, theological perspectives, and ethical exhortations. Yet while recognizing these connections, Lieu does not default to them but instead insists on interpreting the writings on their own terms. She finds no grounds for thinking that these writings assume knowledge and varying interpretations of the Gospel.

Rather, each writing draws on and interprets some shared traditions independently.

While recognizing how central the notion of a community tradition has been in Johannine interpretations, Lieu plots a different path. In her interpretation, each writing offers a distinct and often minimal vision of community. 3 John is the only writing that uses the word "church" (3 Jn 6, 10), although Gaius is not explicitly located in relation to it. It is a place of self-advancement for Diotrephes and exclusion for others, while Demetrius signifies it as a place of welcome. 2 John refers to a house as a location for either true or false teaching (2 Jn 10). From these observations, Lieu is not able to construct a distinctive Johannine community.

First John does not use any distinctive vocabulary for a community although the audience is constructed as a household that is not differentiated by status, ethnicity, religious consciousness, historical self-consciousness, or gender (except for 1 Jn 2:13-14). They are addressed as children and so subordinate to, and dependent on, the author/s. They are to love one another and remain loyal to Jesus. Again, Lieu does not find data from which to construct a distinctive Johannine community.

Lieu has constructed a very different picture of 1–3 John from that described in Chapter 2 and represented by Raymond Brown. Her analysis does not foreground a history of writings associated with the community of the Beloved Disciple. Lieu's discussion emphasizes the individuality of each writing, elaborates the elusiveness of details about the anonymous writers and audiences, teases out tentative details about possible interactions and situations, and concludes that it would be mistaken to take the collection of Johannine writings "as the starting point for the interpretation of any one member." Rather than beginning with assumptions made familiar by previous approaches of, for example, the central role of the Gospel of John; a location and date derivative of the Gospel; a distinctive and unifying Johannine tradition, community, identity, and authorities; and a determining, central event of schism and clearly defined opponents, she insists on engaging each writing on its own terms, seeking to construct its author/s and audience from the minimal clues that she can identify in each one.

Lieu's construction—minimalist compared to Brown's elaborate construction—has proven increasingly convincing for interpreters of these Johannine writings. Lieu is careful not to default to easy or conventional assumptions about the writings, and maintains her commitment to examine each writing as an autonomous work.

Yet this minimalist approach leaves some issues unclear. For example, while Lieu abandons the theory of the writings shaped by John's Gospel and a Johannine community, she recognizes the influence of a Johannine tradition operative in these writings that provides some connection thematically and in vocabulary. It is not evident, though, how she knows of this tradition, which is not the Gospel but seems to exist independently of it.

Lieu does not seem convinced about specific historical settings for 2 and 3 John. For instance, a construction of the elder as a church leader responsible for both letters and for several congregations, including one led by Gaius and one by the "lady," seems plausible. Yet Lieu is reluctant to accept this scenario. Instead, she speculates about the significance of the anonymity of the letters and possible fictional roles of the identified characters that ensure a general address.

Lieu's reading of 1 John 2:18-19, the so-called schism passage, is astute in noticing the operative pronouns. "They" have gone out from "us," the authors, and not from "you," the writing's recipients. This reading certainly decenters the claimed schism and opponents that have often dominated interpretations. Yet the questions concerning the factors shaping the departure and the identity of the opponents don't go away, even if the information is sparse, the departure somewhat distant, and conventions are at hand to fill in the gaps. Nevertheless, the recipients have "heard" about this departure. Consistent with her commitment to read each writing on its own terms, she does not use these opponents to tie the letters together.

Of course, solutions to some issues—for example, the uncertainties of 3 John—are not possible and that recognition informs Lieu's minimalist approach. The consequence is a contribution that is considerable in proposing a significant re-reading of these writings. Where there is no evidence, she refuses to supply assumptions or default to conventions about a purported Johannine tradition or communities.

I find Lieu's approach to be convincing and it will inform the discussion and structure of the rest of this book. Taking seriously her insistence on the autonomy of each of the three writings, I devote Chapters 4–7 to discussion of aspects of 1 John, Chapter 8 to discussion of the much shorter 2 John, and Chapter 9 to discussion of 3 John. I will not attempt to shoehorn them into a purported and linear "Johannine tradition," even while acknowledging some common vocabulary and themes.

Part 2

1 John

4

How Is 1 John Organized?

The organization of 1 John has puzzled interpreters for centuries. While it is referred to as a letter or epistle, it lacks features that we recognize from the beginning and closing sections of Paul's letters. These missing features include naming the writer, the addressees, a greeting or blessing, giving thanks, closing wishes, and farewell. Yet the continual use of the second person plural pronoun, "you," allows the writing to address its audience directly. In this way, it functions like a letter even if does not resemble one.

Almost every interpretive discussion of 1 John acknowledges that there is no agreement concerning the writing's structure or organization. In the sixteenth century, Jean Calvin reportedly claimed that the writing offered no continuous ordering of material. More recently, some interpreters have thought the attempt to map its structure futile and efforts to do so should be abandoned as useless.[1]

Yet most interpreters are intrepid. They plough ahead and add their own analysis of its structure to numerous previous efforts. Some divide the writing into two major sections; others divide it into three or more major sections. Many identify big themes for the sections such as "A Christian ethic, charity/love, and faith;" or "life, truth vs falsehood, the victory of faith;" or "righteousness, love and belief;" or "obedience, love, and faith." These attempts to identify one key theme for each section fail to persuade because the writing's content seems messy with repeated themes popping up in several sections. And naming key themes does not identify an unfolding, coherent, structure for the writing.

Instead of attempting to identify a linear structure, others have suggested that 1 John constructs its content in spirals. Repetitions of themes, cyclic patterns, and the progressive introduction of new ideas constitute the spirals

---

[1]A. E. Brooke, *The Johannine Epistles: A Critical and Exegetical Commentary on the Johannine Epistles* (Edinburgh: T&T Clark, 1912), xxxii.

of arguments. Yet there is no agreement as to what constitutes these spirals and cyclic patterns.

Emerging from these discussions is one common recognition. Most interpreters and commentators observe the importance of the small units that comprise the writing. First John does not comprise long units that develop across many verses. These small units, though, provide interpreters with the big challenge of how to connect the units to each other as well as to the themes that they posit for the larger sections of the writing.

Among these many options, in this chapter, I outline and evaluate three representative attempts to formulate the writing's structure. One approach models itself on an analysis of the Gospel of John. Another approach bases itself in a construction of the situation the writing addresses, identifies a three-section structure, and posits a threefold statement of two important affirmations that the addressees are to embrace. The third approach tracks the writing's argument by attending to the connections of content and rhetoric techniques that draw the subunits together. I find this third option to provide most insight.

Does the Structure of 1 John Imitate the Gospel of John?

One approach has been to see the structure of 1 John as modelled on the Gospel of John. Not surprisingly, since he sees a close relationship between John's Gospel and 1 John, Raymond Brown has adopted this line of thought in appealing to similarities between the two works in structure and thought.[2]

Brown observes that both the Gospel (John 1:1-18) and 1 John (1 Jn 1:1-4) begin with a prologue. The prologues share similarities in vocabulary ("beginning;" "we have looked;" "word;" "life"), in grammatical structures with short clauses and parenthetical interruptions, and a movement of thought from divine initiative and manifestation to human benefit ("receiving life").

Beyond the Prologue, Brown argues that both the Gospel and 1 John have a two-part structure. Part 1 of the Gospel comprises 1:19 to the end of Chapter 12 ("Book of Signs"). This section narrates Jesus's public ministry. Part 1 of 1 John extends in Brown's analysis from 1 John 1:5 to 1 John 3:10.

---

[2]Raymond Brown, *The Epistles of John*. Anchor Bible 30 (Garden City: NYL Doubleday, 1982), 123–8, 764–5.

Brown sees a second section in the Gospel stretching from Chapter 13 to Chapter 20. This "Gospel of Glory" narrates Jesus's farewell discourse to his followers, his passion, and resurrection. In 1 John, this second section begins at 1 John 3:11 and ends in 1 John 5:12. Crucial for Brown's two-part analysis of 1 John is that verse 11 of Chapter 3 employs the same phrase as 1 John 1:5, "this is the message/Gospel." Brown argues that each statement names the theme for the following section, light (1 Jn 1:5–3:10) and love (1 Jn 3:11–5:12).

Brown argues that the light vs darkness theme of Part 1 of 1 John reflects the struggle between two groups. One group comprises the writer's adherents who are addressed as "little children." God is light and these addressees must walk in the light as did Jesus. The second group walks in darkness. It consists of hostile secessionists who have left the community and whom the author attacks viciously as antichrist and liars. These two groups reflect the outsiders/insiders pattern of the Gospel: those who believe in Jesus and those who oppose and kill him. Part 1 of 1 John concludes in 1 John 3:10 by summarizing and contrasting these two groups as "children of God" and "children of the devil." Brown sees this language reflecting the Gospel's division between believing disciples and the unbelieving world under God's judgment (John 3:19-21).

Brown understands Part 2 of 1 John (1 Jn 3:11–5:12) to focus on love. The writing's addressees must love one another as God has loved them in Christ Jesus. Brown argues that this emphasis (1 Jn 3:14, 16) reflects the Gospel's emphasis in the second part on love for other adherents (John 13:34). Brown adds to this concern with love the Gospel's attention to the spirit/paraclete (John 14:17; 16:7-14) which he sees expressed in 1 John 4:3-6 (the spirit of truth versus the spirit of deceit). And, he claims, the reference to blood and water from Jesus's side (John 19:35) informs the three witnesses of spirit, water, and blood in 1 John 5:6-8.

Brown concludes that 1 John's division into two parts at 1 John 1:5 and 1 John 3:11 results from the influence of the organizational structure and thought of the Gospel of John. He goes on to identify subunits within each of the two parts. He determines subunits by grammatical and stylistic features such as:

- subject matter (2:12-14; 2:15-17; 4:1-6)
- repeated phrases (1:6–2:2 "if we say;" 2:4-11 "the person who says;"; 2:29–3:10 "Everyone who;" 5:18-20 "we know"),
- forms of address (2:18 "children;", 2:28 "little children")
- hinge verses (2:27, or 28 or 29; 3:22, 3:23, 3:24; 5:12, 13).

In Part I, Brown identifies five subsections (1:6–2:2; 2:3-11; 2:12-17; 2:18-27; 2:28–3:10). In Part 2, he identifies four (3:12-24; 4:1-6; 4:7–5:4a; 5:4b-12).

In a broad-brush perspective, Brown's focus on the themes of light and love (1 Jn 1:5; 1 Jn 3:11) as reflective of John's Gospel seems helpful. However, on closer inspection, the analysis suffers from selectivity. The Gospel's division into two parts overlooks more nuanced subdivisions such as Chapters 1–4, 5–12, 13–17, 18–21. Brown's claim that light and darkness are central themes in John 1:19–12:48 ignores other dualisms: life and death, from above and from below, God and the devil, and so forth. Nor is the light-darkness theme central to or pervasive in the first part of 1 John. The language of light-darkness appears only in 1 Jn 1:5-7 and 1 Jn 2:8-12. Only two of Brown's six subsections in Part 1 include the light-darkness binary, in fact. And Brown's first section concludes not with the light-darkness dualism but with that of children of God and children of the devil (1 Jn 3:10). Predictably, central to Brown's reading is the role of the schism and the secessionists even though the schism receives little attention in 1 John, the reference to the purported schism in 1 Jn 2:18-19 does not involve light-darkness language, and the Gospel does not narrate an actual schism.

Nor is it evident that 1 Jn 3:11 begins Part 2 of 1 John. Brown notes a repeated formula "This is the message" as signaling this beginning, but 1 John is replete with repeated language and constructions. Brown claims that Part 2's focus on love reflects the Gospel's emphasis. But both the Gospel and 1 John are much more complex than a single theme. For example, love for brothers and sisters is already mentioned in the first part in Chapter 2 of 1 John (1 Jn 2:10).

Brown's analysis highlights, however, the challenges for any attempt to describe the structure of 1 John in terms of central themes to which all the subunits are related. The subunits are not as focused in content nor as related to an overarching theme as Brown's analysis posits.

Two Tests Repeated Three Times

Another approach foregrounds 1 Jn 2:18-19. This passage is understood to describe a schism led by "a leader and his schismatic followers" that the writing's recipients experienced.[3] "As you have heard . . . they went out from

---

3John Painter, *1, 2, and 3 John.* Sacra Pagina 18 (Collegeville: Liturgical Press, 2002), 203.

us, but they did not belong to us." 1 John responds to this threat from false teachings and practices, so this approach claims, by revealing it and setting against it what the author considers to be the truth.

More specifically, this "truth" is expressed in two "tests." According to John Painter, one test is ethical and one Christological. By these means, the recipients might verify whether a person has union or fellowship (*koinōnia*) with God (1 Jn 1:3). These two tests, he argues, are presented in three sections through the document.[4]

The first presentation of the two tests occurs after the prologue in 1:6–2:27. The ethical test—to walk or live in God's light—comprises 1:6–2:17. The Christological test—to have faith in Jesus as the Christ—occupies much less attention in 2:18-27.

The second presentation of the two tests as to whether a person has fellowship or union with God spans 2:28–4:6. The ethical test (2:28–3:24) concerns living a life marked by righteousness or justice, which Painter interprets as "love for the brethren." The "brethren" are other men and women who belong to this community; they do not include outsiders. This "just" or "loving" way of life signifies being born of God; its absence means being born of the devil. Again the Christological test receives less attention in 4:1-6. It comprises a Spirit-inspired confession that Jesus has come in the flesh.

The third presentation of the two tests occurs in 4:7–5:12. Painter sees this section emphasizing the inseparable connection between the two tests. He divides the section into two parts. He does not label the first part as either the ethical or Christological test. Rather, he identifies love as proof of knowing God and being born of God. Love is based on faith (4:7-21). The second part, also not identified as either an ethical or Christological test, is described as identifying faith as the foundation of love (5:1-12).

Verses 13-21 close out Chapter 5 with assurances of confidence in having eternal life and in prayer (5:13-15), of praying for a sinner's repentance (5:16-17), of fellowship with Jesus and God (5:18-20), and a final exhortation to keep themselves away from idols (5:21).

Painter's analysis foregrounds the two tests, ethical and Christological, whereby the addressees might know union or fellowship with God. These

---

[4]Painter's analysis draws on previous discussions that foregrounded the importance of "tests." Theodor Häring, "Gedankengang und Grundgedanke des ersten Johannesbriefes," in *Theologische Abhandlungen Carl von Weizäcker gewidmet* (Freiburg: Mohr, 1892), 171–200; Robert Law, *The Tests of Life: A Study of the First Epistle of St. John* (Edinburgh: T&T Clark, 1909); Brook, *Johannine Epistles*, xxxiv–xxxvii, follows Häring.

emphases are well placed but there are several difficulties. As with most schemes that posit two or three major divisions and assert thematic unity across the writing, the fit is not adequate to the complexity of the writing's content and small units. For example, Painter's naming of the first section highlights light as the central theme, but the vocabulary of "light" appears only in six of thirty-two verses (1 Jn 1:5-7; 2:8-10). The analysis of the third section does not identify the ethical and Christological tests that Painter posits for the first two sections. The section of 5:6-12 that highlights Christological content is not highlighted as a test. The writing's third section has often posed problems for thematic schemes.

And as with most such schemes, connections between the overriding ethical and Christological themes and the numerous subunits that constitute the writing's text are often not clear. For example, it is not clear how the claim of not sinning in 1:8-9 relates to the ethical test. Nor is it clear how the subunits relate to each other. For example, the assurances of 2:12-14 emphasize knowledge more than ethics but then suddenly give way in 2:15-17 to warnings about the world. Numerous other instances of unclear links between units and with the posited overriding themes could be cited.

Taking the Subunits Seriously

Judith Lieu offers a third approach to the structure of 1 John. She proceeds not by identifying two or three major divisions or themes, but by tracking the sequence of thought as it unfolds from subunit to subunit.[5]

The Prologue (1 Jn 1:1-4) introduces the writers ("we") who speak of their particular experience of the revelation of life of the age with God (1 Jn 1:1-2). It also names their goal for the writing. They seek "fellowship" (*koinonia*) or community with "you," the recipients, as well as fellowship with God and Jesus (1 Jn 1:3-4).

Verse 5 introduces a subsection that develops issues related to fellowship with God. It instructs that since God is light, those who claim fellowship with God are to live in (unspecified) appropriate ways (1 Jn 1:6-10). Sin hinders fellowship with God. The reality of sin in the lives of those who claim fellowship with God cannot be denied (1 Jn 1:10). Three "if we say"

---

[5]I follow the discussion and subunits in Judith Lieu, *I, II, III, John: A Commentary* (Louisville: Westminster John Knox, 2008), 35–238.

statements (1 Jn 1:6, 8, 10), along with "if we walk" (1 Jn 1:7), "if we confess" (1 Jn 1:9), and "if anyone sins" (1 Jn 2:1) declarations express the argument. Lieu understands these statements as rhetorical techniques for constructing the argument. She rejects the claims of those who understand them to be polemical attacks on arguments advanced by (theoretical) opponents. Rather, the writers have a pastoral and identity-forming goal in assuring their recipients that God has provided Jesus as an atoning sacrifice for their sin and that with confession sin is forgiven and cleansed (1 Jn 1:7; 2:1-2),

Further consequences of knowing or having fellowship with God, namely love for other believers, are elaborated in the following section (1 Jn 2:3-11). Obedience to the divine commands expressed in love indicates authentic knowing of God. The argument moves forward by paired statements, the repeated "the one who says" statements (1 Jn 2:4, 6, 9) matched with contrasting examples in following verses ("the one who . . .;" 2:5, 10, 11). The concern is with confessions of fellowship with God that are (as they should be) or are not matched by actions of love for a brother or sister. Fellowship with God and "us/you" requires these loving actions. Again there is no evidence of polemics against imaginary opponents who supposedly speak these statements. Rather the verses set out the desired practices and identity of the writing's recipients.

Verses 12-14 sustain the theme of fellowship with God and community members by recapitulating content from the previous sections. Repetition provides assurance for the recipients. Sin is forgivable (1 Jn 2:12), God is known (1 Jn 2:13a, 14a), and victory over the evil one is won (1 Jn 2:13b, 14b). The recipients have aligned themselves with God and know fellowship with God in the context of "darkness." This "darkness" is now identified as the devil who opposes God. Immediately with this naming of the evil one, verses 15-17 warn about the attraction of "the world" defined in verse 16 as the desire of flesh and eyes and pride in riches. In this context of hostility to God, the writers guard against complacency by exhorting the recipients not to love the world but to stand firm in obedient loyalty to God (1 Jn 2:15, 17).

Having emphasized authentic confession and living, and exhorted faithfulness in the context of evil, the writer now alludes to a situation of threat and division that "we" have experienced and about which "you" have heard. The writer refers to this situation with language that constructs it as a final eschatological conflict ("last hour") between opponents of God who deny the Father and the Son ("antichrists,") and those loyal to God (1 Jn 2:18-23). The recipients are warned not to succumb to this deceit but are to be confident, assured in and faithful to both the truth and the anointing that they have received until Jesus's coming (1 Jn 2:24-8).

More assurances follow concerning the addressees' identity and way of life (1 Jn 2:29–3:12). They are grounded in God's begetting of God's children. This identity is expressed in doing justice. God's children are contrasted with those born of the devil whose identity and deeds (not doing justice; not loving brothers and sisters) are antithetical to God. Accordingly, the addressees are exhorted not to be deceived but to do justice (1 Jn 3:7-10). Living a life of justice and love marks them as children of God (1 Jn 3:10b-12).

The section of 1 John 2:29–3:12 is structured on a series of "everyone who" statements that emphasize a moral dualism contrasting the identities and deeds of God's children who do justice and the children of the devil who sin: doing justice or sinning (1 Jn 2:29b, 3:4a), indwelling him or sinning (1 Jn 3:6a, 6b); doing justice or sinning (1 Jn 3:7b, 8a); born of God or not doing justice (1 Jn 3:9a, 10b).

This dualism and the recognition of the world's hatred (1 Jn 3:13) prepares for a contrasting and encouraging emphasis on love within the community as participation in life of the age (1 Jn 3:14-24). The opposite of love for brothers and sisters is "death," hatred, and murder (1 Jn 3:14b-15). Love for brothers and sisters imitates God's self-giving love in providing the world's goods for them when they are in need (1 Jn 3:16-18). Verses 19-24 develop this emphasis from relationships with brothers and sisters, to confidence before God gained by obeying the commandment to believe in Jesus Christ and love brothers and sisters (1 Jn 3:23).

After encouraging the addressees, the author now warns them. He exhorts them to be vigilant in a confusing context that requires discerning competing Spirits (1 Jn 4:1-6). False prophets and antichrists originate a false spirit that does not confess Jesus ("has come in the flesh;" 1 Jn 4:1, 3). This false spirit poses a serious challenge for deception but the addressees can be confident because of their greater resources. They know God's Spirit, who inspires the true confession that Jesus shared their humanity. Their identity as God's children is affirmed; they originate from God who is greater than the world, thereby they can discern the spirit of truth and of error (1 Jn 4:1-6).

The writer returns to his (?) emphasis on God's love (1 Jn 4:7–5:4). The section intertwines God's relationship with believers, believers with God, and relationship of believers with one another. The tone is explanatory and encouraging. Verses 7-10 celebrate God's love, revealed in God sending Jesus as an atoning sacrifice for sin. This love is the source for believers to love one another and experience fellowship ("abiding") with

God (1 Jn 4:11-16). This love drives out fear and provides boldness even for the day of judgment (1 Jn 4:17-19). It is expressed in love for God and in obedience to God's commandment in loving the brothers and sisters. Failing to love exposes one as a liar.

Several emphases from the previous verses—conquering the world (1 Jn 4:4-5); right belief (1 Jn 4:2-3, 15; 5:1)—again come to the fore but now as resources for overcoming the world (1 Jn 5:4-13). Believing that Jesus is the Son of God and receiving God's testimony that Jesus is the Son enables the believer to conquer the world. To reject God's testimony is to make God a liar (1 Jn 5:10). The Son is important because God has given new life of the age in the Son. To "have the Son" is to have life (1 Jn 5:11-12). This life-giving relationship with God and Jesus is the "fellowship" that the writer seeks with the addressees in the opening verses (1 Jn 1:3).

The writer provides concluding assurances about this life, first by stating the purpose of his writing which is to secure their belief in the Son and their experience of life of the age (1 Jn 5:13). Further, this assurance results in boldness before God (1 Jn 5:14). Yet immediately the writer returns to the threat of sin to this assurance and communal experience of participation in God's life (1 Jn 5:15-17). He addresses sin's threat with three concluding "we know" affirmations or communal certainties that carry certain implications (1 Jn 5:18, 19, 20): those born of God do not sin but there is protection against the devil; the addressees are God's children and not under the power of the evil one; the addressees are committed to God and God's son Jesus Christ in whom is life of the age. These three affirmations conclude the writing's construction of an imagined community that is in fellowship with God and the writer, and that shares the victory won by God's son over all opposition to God.

Yet, as the final verse acknowledges, the victory is contested (1 Jn 5:21). The writing has identified alternatives to and opponents of this community from antichrist, false prophets, the devil, the world, falsehood, death, and darkness. The final verse summarizes these threats with the archetypal biblical image of "idols" that represent false loyalties. The writing concludes with an exhortation to maintain fellowship with "us" and the Father and Son. Implicit is a warning of what will be lost if they fail to do so.

I have summarized Lieu's discussion in some detail to demonstrate her approach to the writing's structure. Instead of seeking to identify two or three large sections and their overarching themes, Lieu focuses on the subunits. Her attention is on the thematic, verbal, and stylistic links that draw the subunits together in order to show how the writing's thought wobbles and unfolds from one unit to the next, sometimes repeating and amplifying previous emphases, sometimes adding new ones.

Rhetorical Analysis

Duane Watson's rhetorical analysis also sets aside the pursuit of major divisions and overarching themes as the key to the structure of 1 John. He also focuses on the writing's subunits.[6] Whereas Lieu's focus falls more on the content and stylistic expression of the unfolding argument, Watson's concern is with the rhetorical techniques that link units and express the argument both between and within units.

Watson argues that 1 John is not polemic against opponents, but is epideictic rhetoric. The goal of epideictic rhetoric is to strengthen the recipients' adherence to the Gospel values and faith that they already hold, namely fellowship and life with the writer and with God and Jesus (1 Jn 1:3). The rhetoric upholds and praises these commitments while contrasting them with, and blaming, those who oppose them: false prophets, antichrists, the world.

Watson demonstrates that the rhetorical technique of amplification pervades the subunits and is fundamental to the writer's construction of his argument. Drawing on rhetorical handbooks, especially Cicero and Quintilian, Watson identifies some twenty variants of the technique of amplification. While some techniques overlap, identifying them provides insight into how the writing's arguments are structured and developed from one short unit to another.

Space limits prevent a discussion of every variant and example that Watson cites. The following discussion identifies some of the main rhetorical techniques that elaborate the argument and draw subunits together.

- *Strong words*: these words substitute for and amplify previous words. For example, "all who hate a brother or sister are murderers" (1 Jn 3:15). In this example, the term "murderers" amplifies the vice of those who "hate" a brother or sister. Here the technique employs exaggeration or *hyperbole* in moving from hate to murder.

---

[6]Duane Watson, "Amplification Techniques in I John: The Interaction of Rhetorical Style and Invention," *JSNT* 51 (1993): 99–123.

- *Augmentation*: the argument moves by stepping up, intensifying, or expanding the claim. In 1 John 2:2, Jesus is the atoning sacrifice "for our sins . . . but also for the sins of the whole world." The claim about the impact of Jesus's death expands from "us" to "the whole world." In 1 John 3:20, God is not only "greater than our hearts" but further, God "knows everything." The expansion reassures the addressees of their commitments to a powerful and trustworthy God.

- *Comparison*: this technique effects amplification by gradation, moving from the lesser to the greater. In 1 John 3:2, the addressees are "God's children now" but in the future "we will be like him for we will see him as he is." In 1 John 5:9, a comparison between receiving human testimony and divine testimony elevates the latter as greater and more reliable.

- *Accumulation*: words or phrases of identical meaning are amassed to strengthen the argument. In 1 John 1:1-3, the revelation of life is "heard . . . seen . . . looked at . . . touched." In 1 John 2:16, the world is defined as "the desire of the flesh . . . of the eyes, the pride in riches."

- *Expolitio*: this term denotes various forms of repetition. One form is to restate the same idea. In 1 John 1:2, "this life was revealed . . . (it) was revealed to us." Another form is to present the idea in different language. In 1 John 5:2-3, "obeying" his commandments is expressed as "doing" and "keeping" them. In 1 John 2:16, "not from the Father" is to be "not from the world." Another form repeats the idea with a contrast. In 1 John 2:23, whoever denies the son does not have the Father but to confess the son is to have the Father. In 1 John 2:27, the anointing's teaching "is true and is not a lie." In 1 John 4:6, those who know God "listen to us" whereas "whoever is not from God does not listen to us."

- *Regressio*: this form of amplification reiterates what is known but introduces a distinction. In 1 John 2:18 "you have heard that antichrist is coming." The verse continues by modifying what has been known by rendering "antichrist" now as a plural ("antichrists") and changing the time referent from future to present: "so now many antichrists have come."

- *Conduplicatio*: common in 1 John, and often noted by interpreters, is the amplification of a theme by the repetition of key words and phrases. In 1 John 2:12-14, repeated are the verbs "write," "know," and "conquer," and the nouns "fathers" and "young people." In 1 John 2:15-17, "world" is repeated. In 1 John 2:18, "last hour" is repeated. There are many more examples.

- *Synonymy*: this technique uses synonyms to emphasize a claim. Again there are many examples including two words for "see" and "looked at" (1 John 1:1), "commandment" and "word" (1 John 2:7), "sin" and "lawlessness" (1 John 3:4).
- *Epanaphora*: this technique employs repeated phrases to introduce material. In 1 John 1:6, 8, 10, each claim begins "if we say." And "the one who says" introduces 1 John 2:4, 6, 9. In 1 John 3:3-4, the repeated "everyone who" contrasts the faithful and unfaithful. The writing concludes in 1 John 5:18-20 with a threefold "we know" to emphasize the addressees' knowledge.
- *Commoratio*: this common technique amplifies key topics by highlighting different dimensions of them. In 1 John 1:5–2:2, sin recurs in relation to various topics such as self-deception, confession, forgiveness, Jesus's sacrifice, the world's sinfulness. The frequent return to confessions in the writing about Jesus as the Christ or come in the flesh, and the command to love brothers and sisters are further examples.
- *Antithesis*: this technique, also commonly recognized, creates the writing's pervasive dualisms: walking in the light or darkness (1 Jn 1:6-7), children of God or children of the devil (1 Jn 3:1-8), two spirits (1 Jn 4:2-3), from God or from the world (1 Jn 4:4-5), believing or not believing in God (1 Jn 5:10). *Antitheses* can be sustained over longer passages such as 1 John 1:6-7, 8-9, 10–2:1-2; 2:4-5, 6-8, 9-11, and 1 John 2:29b; 3:4a, 3:6a-6b; 3:7b-8a; 3:9a-10b. The antitheses amplify acceptable behavior and identity for the addressees as "children of God."
- *Personification*: this technique attributes agency or an action to an entity that is not a person. The "blood of Jesus cleanses" (1 Jn 1:7); Spirit, water and blood testify (1 Jn 5:7-8).

These and other rhetorical techniques pervade the writing. It is in these details in the subunits that the writing formulates its claims and does its identity-constructing work. These techniques of amplification and repetition ensure the writing's message, themes, and topics are clearly connected, expressed, and emphasized. Employing these rhetorical techniques allows the writer to strengthen the addressees' commitment to what they already know and to what the writer deems to be the truth.

Watson's approach, allied with Lieu's work, suggests that an important key to 1 John's structure lies not in identifying two or three major sections and overarching themes but in attending to the content, style, and rhetorical techniques that connect the subunits and effect the writing's communication as epideictic rhetoric. This rhetoric strengthens the recipients' adherence to the Gospel values, namely fellowship and life with the writer and with God and Jesus (1 Jn 1:3).

5

Does 1 John Attack Opponents?

Two Approaches: Polemic or Pastoral?

In the last chapter, I referred to 1 John as epideictic rhetoric. Through the next couple of chapters, I will elaborate dimensions of this rhetoric that strengthens the recipient's adherence to Gospel values and faith. In this chapter, I address the question of the writing's audience; to whom is it directed?

One interpretation of 1 John understands it to be a polemical writing that attacks opponents of the Jesus-believers.[1] This approach sees 1 John 2:18-23, with its reference to a "schism" in which secessionists "went out from us," as central to understanding the writing and its context. Interpreters try to identify these opponents and their views by mirror-reading the writing's claims. Whatever the writing declares, or resists, is understood in this view to be polemic against and rebuttal of the opponents. While interpreters make various suggestions about the identity of these opponents, there is no agreement.

Another interpretation plays down these polemical, schismatic, and secessionist dimensions. It understands the writing to have a more pastoral,

---

[1] Among many discussions of the opponents or secessionists, the following have been especially informative: Raymond Brown, *The Community of the Beloved Disciple: The Life, Loves, and Hates of an Individual Church in New Testament Times* (New York: Paulist, 1979), 93–144; John Painter, "The 'Opponents' in I John," *New Testament Studies* 32 (1986): 48–71; Judith Lieu, *I, II, & III John: A Commentary* (Louisville: Westminster John Knox, 2008); Daniel Streett, *They Went Out From Us: The Identity of the Opponents in First John.* BZNW 177 (Berlin: de Gruyter), 2011.

rather than polemical, function in assuring and encouraging the addressees as Jesus-believers to live faithfully in the midst of a hostile world opposed to God's purposes. The "world" is dangerous because in it live figures ("antichrists," "false prophets," "liars") who are hostile toward, and opponents of, God and God's children. This approach (epideictic rhetoric) understands these terms as referring more to representative rather than specific figures, recognizes very few verses in the writing that refer to "opponents," and is not much interested in identifying specific opponents.

The differences between the two approaches center on reading strategies; polemics vs. pastoral; maximalist mirror-reading vs. minimalist reading; confident reconstructions vs. caution; 1 John 2:19 as central or peripheral; specific identification of the opponents vs. representative figures.

The maximalist, polemical, mirror-reading understands the writing to reflect accurately the situation that it addresses. So it interprets the affirmations that 1 John makes as reflecting and rejecting the challenges, errors, and identity of the opponents. The approach appeals to a central cluster of texts such as 1 John 2:19 (secessionists and schism), 4:1-6 and 2 Jn 7 (Christological issues denying Jesus's flesh), and 1 John 5:6 (denying Jesus's human identity). Beyond these texts, interpreters add a range of further verses. So, for example, the recognitions of sin in 1 John 1:6-10, disobedience in 2:4-8, and lack of love for brothers and sisters (2:9-11) are understood to show that the opponents were ethically deficient. On this approach, any affirmation can be understood as reflecting and refuting claims of the opponents. So the affirmation at 1 John 3:1 that the addressees are "children of God" can be interpreted to reflect either the opponents' claim to and/or denial of this identity. The uncontrolled attributing of content to opponents is a major weakness of the maximalist-polemical approach.

Minimalist-pastoral approaches exercise much more restraint and caution in looking for explicit identifiers of any opponents. They recognize, in fact, that references to any opponents are few and vague in detail. The first reference does not occur until well into the writing at 1 John 2:18-19, and after the opening chapter and a half that have been so overinterpreted by maximalist approaches. The rhetoric is focused on the addressees much more than any opponents, so it is pastoral in encouraging and affirming the audience rather than polemical in countering opponents.

Having identified these methodological differences, I first discuss five unconvincing identifications for the opponents that the polemical approaches have suggested. Then I turn to the minimalist, pastoral approach. I find the latter more convincing.

The Opponents are Gnostics?

A long-standing scholarly tradition identifies the opponents of 1 John as Gnostics. Attempts to define or describe Gnostics are challenging because they were not a monolithic tradition. The opponents are constructed as denying the physicality of Jesus's existence, whether his incarnation (1 Jn 1:1; 4:2-3), and/or the reality of his death (1 Jn 2:2; 5:6-7). From this denial the conclusion is drawn that they must be Gnostics, since Gnostics regarded matter as evil. They are also constructed as immoral or libertines who claimed that since they were the seed of God, they did not need to keep God's commandments or express love (1 Jn 1:6; 2:1-6, 9-11; 2:29–3:10; 5:17). They are also said to claim sinlessness (1:8, 10), that God comprised light and darkness (1:5), and that salvation came from their knowledge of the cosmos and their own identity and not from Jesus's atoning death (1:6-7; 2:2). Their elite status deriving from their anointing, not the teaching of Jesus, guided their actions (2:20, 27; 3:24; 4:1-6; 5:6-8). They emphasized a realized eschatology and denied future judgment (2:28). They charged apostles with corrupting the teaching of Jesus (1:1-3; 2:13-14, 24).

This summary exhibits the method of maximum mirror-reading whereby the writing's affirmations are understood to reject the claims of these purported Gnostic opponents. Yet the approach has three challenges. One is that it is not clear by what criteria verses are determined to be polemical. Second, the claim is anachronistic since Gnostics emerge, it seems, in the mid-second century, after the likely time of writing of 1 John. Third, there is much debate about how to define Gnosticism and to identify its defining characteristics when it does emerge. Recent scholarship has established that Gnosticism was not monolithic and that some of the standard claims made about Gnostics (opposed to the material world; ethically deficient; spiritually superior) cannot be generalized to all Gnostics. These factors disqualify the attempt to identify the opponents as Gnostics.

The Opponents are Cerinthians?

Cerinthians (not a typo for Corinthians!) were followers of a prophetic figure called Cerinthus. According to advocates of this identification, Cerinthians advocated a separationist Christology which understood "Jesus" to be a first-century (human) Jew while "Christ" was a divine spiritual being or son of God. Christ descended on Jesus at baptism but departed before the cross and returned to heaven. They therefore denied the confession that *Jesus* is the Christ and Son of God. The polemic of 1 John 2:22 against denying Jesus is the Christ is understood to identify the Cerinthians as liars and antichrists. Likewise, the confession of 1 John 4:2-3 that Jesus Christ came in the flesh is understood to counter the Cerinthian claim that Christ did not stay in the flesh of the crucified Jesus. And 1 John 5:6-7 also rejects this Cerinthian claim by affirming the death ("blood") of Jesus Christ. Other verses that affirm the identification of Jesus and Christ are understood to reflect and reject Cerinthian claims (1 Jn 4:15; 1 Jn 5:1, 5). So too does the double name Jesus Christ in 1:3; 2:1; 3:23; 4:2; 5:6, 20.

This identification of the opponents as Cerinthians is also unconvincing. As with Gnostics, this identification suffers from being anachronistic. The earliest reference to Cerinthus comes from the 140s, perhaps several decades after 1 John was probably written. Further, reconstructions of Cerinthianism suffer from a lack of reliable and consistent sources. Irenaeus, for example, late in the second century, is the earliest source for the Christology that separates Jesus and Christ (*Adv. Haer.* 1.26.1), yet subsequently he presents Cerinthus as a gnostic (*Adv. Haer.* 3.11.1). Moreover, if 1 John is supposed to be polemic against Cerinthianism, it is muddly and ineffective at best. There is no discussion of the meaning of "Christ." The claim of 1 John 4:2 that Jesus Christ came in the flesh does not negate Cerinthianism because the latter would agree that Jesus and Christ were united in the flesh from baptism for a period of time up to the crucifixion. Likewise, 1 John 5:6 can be read as agreeing with the Cerinthians if the mention of "water" refers to baptism. That would leave only the reference to Jesus's death ("blood") as refutation. These factors disqualify the attempt to identify the opponents as Cerinthians.

The Opponents Are Docetists?

This identification has had considerable support. It understands Docetists variously to deny Jesus's humanity and physicality, and/or to claim that his humanity and suffering had no salvific value and/or that he only seemed to suffer and be human (e.g. Ignatius, *Smyrnaeans* 5:2; 7:1; *Magnesians* 11; *Trallians* 9:1; 10). Its emphasis on Jesus's divinity could not be reconciled with Jesus's humanity.

Interpreters who construe the opponents as Docetists read the affirmation of 1 John 4:2-3 and 2 Jn 7 that Jesus came in the flesh as polemic. Using a mirror-reading approach, they understand the affirmation to reflect the Docetists' denial of Jesus's humanity. Likewise the references in 1 John 5:6 to Jesus's coming "by water and blood" are understood to affirm his birth and death against Docetist denials of Jesus's physical existence. Other references such as 1 John 1:2, read in relation to Jesus and not testimony about eternal life, stress the visibility, tangibility and physicality of the incarnation. And the affirmations concerning Jesus's atoning death in 1 John 1:7 and 2:2 are understood to combat Docetist denials of his suffering and death.

Despite its relative popularity, this identification of the opponents as Docetists fails to convince. The writing's only reference to some who "went out from us" (1 Jn 2:19) includes nothing docetic. Nor do subsequent references to denying the Father and the Son (2:22-5). The reference to Jesus "has come in the flesh" (1 Jn 4:2; 2 Jn 7) could be anti-docetic but if so, it is a solitary reference in 1 John and occurs only in the last part of the writing. The writing does not employ obvious means of refutation such as rehearsing accounts of Jesus's birth or his deeds of healing and feeding or his crucifixion and resurrection appearances. Common vocabulary that might echo Docetic concerns—such as the verb "seem" and the noun "body"—are not used, while the noun "flesh" occurs only in 1 John 4:2.

The Opponents Are Misinterpreters of John's Gospel?

This view, advocated by Raymond Brown and numerous followers, has dominated recent constructions of the opponents in recent decades. Brown constructs the opponents as so emphasizing Jesus's divine principle and pre-existence that they devalue Jesus's human existence. While they recognize his humanity as real (they are not Docetists), they did not find it salvifically significant (1 Jn 1:1-3; 2:18-27; 4:1-6; 5:6-11; 2 Jn 7–9). They downplayed the centrality of Jesus's atoning death and life to prefer salvation by revelation (1 Jn 1:7; 2:2; 3:16; 4:10). In addition, they are constructed as claiming to be sinless (1 Jn 1:6, 8, 10), failing to observe the commandments (1 Jn 2:3-4; 3:22, 24; 5:2-3), and not loving their brothers and sisters in the community (1 Jn 2:9-11; 3:11-18, 22-4; 4:19–5:3). Brown's maximalist mirror-reading is especially evident when he claims that 1 John corrects the opponents' over-realized eschatology by introducing reminders of future eschatological accountability (1 Jn 2:28; 3:2) and ethical responsibility (1 Jn 2:28; 3:3; 4:17). Throughout, Brown argues that the opponents have misinterpreted elements in John's Gospel to arrive at these false confessions.

Brown's influential construction is susceptible, however, to a number of objections. His maximalist mirror-reading strategy is to the fore as he constantly reads any statement in the writing as polemic that refutes claims he assumes the opponents made. Yet 1 John does not present its content as the claims of the opponents. How does Brown know that 1 John is a pervasive polemic?

Likewise, if the opponents are misinterpreting John's Gospel as Brown claims, why does 1 John not cite and address any of the misinterpreted Gospel texts to correct the error? In appealing to the Gospel of John, Brown supplies a framework for 1 John that 1 John itself does not evoke or employ. And if the secessionists deny that Jesus's ministry was salvifically insignificant, why does the writing not counter this claim repeatedly and with examples from Jesus's ministry? If the statement that Jesus has come in the flesh (1 Jn 4:2) is supposed to refute this central claim of the opponents, why does it not appear until Chapter 4 and only there? Brown's construction seems somewhat contradictory in denying any salvific significance for Jesus's life, yet he asserts that the opponents see it as having some revelatory importance. And why would the opponents be so obviously ethically deficient in advocating a lack of love for community members when the Gospel explicitly and unambiguously commands such love (John 13:34-5; 15:12-14)? This construction lacks support and control with its extensive mirror-reading strategy and polemical function.

The Opponents No Longer Affirm Jesus as the Messiah?

This approach identifies the opponents as Jews who had previously confessed Jesus as the Messiah but have now, for whatever reason, abandoned that confession, left the Jesus-community, and returned to the synagogue (1 Jn 2:18-23). They are identified as many antichrists who "went out from us." They deny "that Jesus is the Christ" and in denying the son as the Messiah, they deny God as Father. The denial of Jesus as Messiah repudiates a central confession in the Johannine tradition (John 20:31).

The writer of 1 John sets their departure in eschatological perspective as rebellion against God. They are deemed "antichrists" and it is the "last hour" when opposition to God increases and apostates and apostasy become increasingly visible before the final and full establishment of the divine reign (e,g, Mark 13; Rev. 13; 2 Thess. 2:9-11).

The writer explains to the recipients that the departure of these antichrists indicates that they never "belonged to us" (1 Jn 2:19). They exemplify the false, the liars. Then the writer assures the recipients that *they* have "anointing" which provides them with the knowledge that they need to remain in the truth that Jesus is the Messiah, and to understand the nature of the departure of these apostates as part of eschatological rebellion (1 Jn 2:20-1). Abiding in the proclamation they heard from the beginning means, in contrast to those who departed, remaining loyal to Jesus as Messiah and therefore to God with the reward of eternal life (1 Jn 2:24-7).

What role do two other frequently evoked passages (1 Jn 4:1-6; 1 Jn 5:6) play? Neither passage explicitly identifies opponents. In 4:1, the reference to "false prophets [who] have gone out into the world" is said to refer to different figures, namely itinerant prophets and not to those who have left the Jesus-believers in 1 Jn 2:19. They are not said to have left "us" and are not identified as formerly belonging to the recipients' community. The reference to Jesus "come in the flesh" is read as expressing the basic confession of 1 Jn 2:22 that Jesus is the Messiah. The confession that Jesus has come in the flesh is a confession found in other Christian writings and refers to the span of Jesus's human existence (Rom. 1:3-4; 8:3; 9:5; 1 Tim. 3:16).

Likewise, the reference to the three witnesses of water, blood, and spirit in I.5:6 is not presented as polemic against opponents. Rather it is understood as an exhortation to the recipients to continue to live faithfully to the testimony from God about Jesus. The three witnesses attest Jesus's messiahship demonstrated in his baptism, death, and through the spirit present among the recipients.

In contrast to the four previous hypotheses that employ maximalist mirror-reading and polemical strategies, clearly this option takes a more minimal approach. It appeals only to the one explicit textual reference to opponents in 1 Jn 2:19-22. Separating 1 Jn 2:19-22 from 4:1-2, those who departed and the false prophets in the world, is an uncommon move in the discussions about opponents but it does highlight differences, rather than continuities, between the two passages. Also distinctive is the interpretation of "come in the flesh" (1 Jn 4:2; 2 Jn 7) as a conventional confession of Jesus's human existence and not as polemic against claims of opponents.

That being said, the claim that the opponents or secessionists are Jews who are returning to the synagogue has no support from the writing. Jewish converts were not the only ones confessing Jesus as Messiah. Gentiles in the Jesus-movement could also make this confession in understanding Jesus to be anointed by God as God's agent and son. And the writing does not name the synagogue as anyone's origin or destination. The claim that some departed in order to return to a synagogue is unsustainable.

The Opponents Are Not the Main Point?

None of these five attempts to read 1 John as a polemic directed against an identifiable and specific group of opponents has carried the day. It is not clear why a polemical reading is required, and none of the suggested target groups fits the letter's content.

The following section develops an alternative approach that I find more persuasive. Its methodological stance rejects what seems to be the overconfidence that has so often marked the mirror-reading quest to identify the opponents. It eschews a polemical approach and decenters a quest to identify specific "opponents." Instead, it embraces uncertainty, rejects unsupported assumptions, and recognizes the sorts of weaknesses identified in these five options. It frames 1 John not primarily as polemic against secessionist opponents but pastoral toward the writing's recipients. In this approach, references to "opponents" are constructed to reinforce the writing's affirmation by contrast and dissent.

In support of this quite different orientation is the enigmatic report of the departure of the so-called "secessionist opponents" in 1 Jn 2:18-19. This first reference to the departure does not occur until one-third of the way into the writing which suggests that the so-called schism—whatever it might be— may not be central to the writing. And while the reference is long on theological-eschatological interpretation ("last hour;" "antichrists"), it is short on specifics about whatever happened (Who? Single or protracted event? Local or general? How many departed? Expelled or voluntary departure? Bitter or respectful? Uniform or multiple motivations etc.). The eschatological language interprets the division in cosmic terms as part of the intensified opposition to God that was expected to mark the final conflict between those loyal to God and those opposed, here, to Christ (1 Thess. 5:1-11; 2 Thess. 2:1-12; Mark 13:22). Other New Testament texts stereotypically warn of coming opponents and false teachers as the eschaton approaches (1 Tim. 4:1-5; 2 Tim. 3:8-9; 2 Pet. 2:1-22; 3:3; Jude 17–19).

Verse 19 does not identify the issue in dispute. That the departure involved Christological claims which now have been abandoned and/or rejected could be inferred from labeling the departees as "antichrists." Moreover, the successive verses in 1 John 2:22-4 emphasize that confession of Jesus as Christ involves recognizing Jesus as the son or agent of God the Father. To reject this confession is to be a liar. It must be remembered, however, that the writing does not make it explicit that the opponents denied the confession. The term "anti-Christ" could be generalized to denote anyone opposed to the Jesus group for any reason.

More important, though, is an observation that overturns this approach. Significantly, as Lieu highlights, details in the wording of 2:18-19 have often been overlooked in attempted reconstructions and identifications. The assumption has commonly been made that the opponents have gone out from those addressed by the writing.

But Lieu's careful reading notes the differentiated pronouns of "you and "us" in 2:18-19. First in verse 18, the addressees ("you") are said to "have heard" that antichrist/s have and are coming. "You" have "heard" about the antichrists because those who departed left "us," not "you." Verse 18 indicates that the "antichrists" left the writers, and did not leave those addressed by 1 John. The recipients have heard about this departure but did not themselves experience the departure.

Second, verse 19 confirms this scenario by repeating the pronoun "us" five times. The repetition emphasizes that the departure was from "us," the writers, but not from "you," the recipients of 1 John:

They went out from *us*
They were not from *us*
If they were from *us*, they would have remained with *us*
. . . that all were not from *us*.

This contrast of pronouns has marked the writing since the opening three verses of Chapter 1 in which "*we*" hope that "*you* might have fellowship with *us*" (1 Jn 1:3). Here the recipients ("you") have not experienced the departure of or schism with the secessionists that "we" the writers have experienced.

Accordingly, the writer/s is/are not focused on settling scores with opponents and proving them wrong with a sustained polemic. The writing does not attack and correct recipients who have strayed from the truth and need to be restored. Rather, it seeks to secure the loyalties and commitments of the recipients of the writing in a threatening "world" in which reside those who are hostile toward God and the divine purposes (1 Jn 4:5-6). The recipients are reassured that they have an anointing that keeps them in the truth and faithful even if others expose themselves as not true believers by leaving the writer's community (1 Jn 2:24-8).

How, then, are the other texts commonly used to construct opponents interpreted in this approach?

The addressees are directly addressed in 1 Jn 4:1-2. They are warned about "false prophets" in the hostile world, alerted to the task of discerning spirits, and urged to be faithful to the spirit of God that confesses Jesus has come in the flesh. The denial of this confession is typical of antichrists in the dualistic world that the writing constructs (1 Jn 4:3). Are the "false prophets" of 4:1 the same as the antichrists who went out from "us" in 2:19? The identifier, "false prophets," draws partly on prophetic traditions in which false prophets are identified as those who claim to speak a word from God but lack legitimate authority and accurate speech as lying teachers (e.g. Jer. 23:28-32). They also partly draw on the same eschatological framework as that of 1 John 2:19. The verse constructs them as stereotypical figures that belong to and represent the increased hostility toward the divine purposes and loyalists that mark the approaching culmination of those purposes. They share the same confession-denying quality that the antichrists exhibit (1 Jn 2:22; 4:3). Yet these prophets are not identified as leaving the believing community.

Moreover, mitigating any attempt to identify these false prophets as specific opponents is the focus of 1 Jn 4:1-6 on the recipients. The writer affirms in the context of "false prophets . . . in the world" the greater resources and qualities that the addressees have that will enable them to remain true to their identity as "children of God" (1 Jn 4:4). They have the Spirit of God. They are from God. They are conquerors of the hostile world. They can recognize the false prophets because they do not listen to them as children of God. They know the division of truth and error. The section is pastoral addressed to 1 John's recipients rather than polemical in attacking opponents.

And the confession of 1 John 4:2 that Jesus has come in the flesh? The confession is that of the addressees, inspired by the Spirit of God. It affirms the identity of Jesus as the Messiah who has come and shared humanity. The phrase "in the flesh" signifies his presence not only in the human sphere, even in a contestive one often opposed to God (2:16), but especially present among the addressees who confess him, obey the commandments and so belong to God. The focus rests on the addressees not the opponents.

Similarly, the claim of 1 John 5:6 that Jesus "came by water and blood" concerns the addressees and not opponents. No antichrists or false prophets are mentioned. To the fore is the addressees' right belief pertaining to Jesus Christ. He has been affirmed as Messiah and Son (1 Jn 2:22-3) who has come among humanity (1 Jn 4:2). Now this belief or faith in Jesus as Son of God is promoted as the means of conquering "the world," all that resists God (1 Jn 5:4-5). This Son came "by water and blood," understood variously as Christological indicators of his human appearing, namely conception and birth, baptism and death, and/or as soteriological indicators of the benefits he provides to believers, namely life ("water," baptism?) and forgiveness ("blood," 1 Jn 1:7; 2:2). Through these experiences, God and the Spirit testify to the Son in whom the recipients believe (1 Jn 5:9). Again, the consequence of this affirmation of belief is a dualistic division. Those who refuse are named liars; those who believe the testimony have eternal life (1 Jn 5:10-12).

And the other texts that are commonly evoked to refer to opponents? How to read, for example, the "If we say" (1 Jn 1:6, 8, 10), "everyone who" (1 Jn 2:23; 3:4, 6, 9, 15) and "the one who says/does/knows" (1 Jn 2:4, 6, 9; 3:7-8; 4:6) sayings? Despite the imagination of various scholars, the sayings do not identify any opponents. More importantly, the section (1 Jn 1:5–2:11) develops the thought from verse 5's affirmation that God is light and without darkness. Yet those who confess allegiance to God know sinful actions that fail to embody the divine light. The passage addresses the problem of sin among the recipients. It recognizes that there is no denying the presence of sin—"If we say that we have no sin …." "Whoever says, 'I have come to know him' but does not obey his commandments …."—yet it also affirms both that Jesus Christ provides forgiveness (1 Jn 1:9; 2:1-2) as well as requiring obedience to binding ethical demands (1 Jn 2:5, 9-10). The passage is pastoral not polemical in offering instruction and exhortation. Its addressees are not opponents but the writing's recipients. The same arguments can be made throughout the writing.

Lieu comments:[2]

> The author's concern consistently is *not* with what is going on outside but with the internal commitment and adherence of those to whom the letter is written. He does not engage in attacking positions held by others but focuses on exploring the implications of those already held by himself and his readers. It is they who can say they have known God and love God (1 Jn 2:3, 13-14; 5:2); it is they who in some circumstances may be able to say they do not sin…. His questioning, hypothesizing style (1:6, "If we say;" 2:9, "The one who says") is designed to engage his readers and to draw them inevitably toward the position that he holds. Even his Christological assertions are concerned with what must be said, not with any alternative view held by others, and they can be seen to hold firm to a point—that the Son of God really did fulfill his mission in human form in the person of Jesus …

Conclusion

Interpreters have for many years debated the identity of the purported opponents or secessionists mentioned in one verse of 1 John. Foundational to the debate is the issue of method: how do we know anything about these

---

[2]Lieu, *I, II, & III John*, 11.

opponents? Mirror-reading is a common strategy whereby the writing's numerous claims are understood to refute teachings of the opponents, thereby revealing their identity. But a major weakness of this approach is its conjectural nature and lack of controls. How do interpreters decide what is or is not a claim from the opponents?

An alternative method has not adopted a mirror-reading approach. It has not made 1 John 2:19-23 the center for interpreting the whole writing. Instead, it has understood the writing to have a pastoral function in its address to its recipients; rather than serving as a polemical attack on opponents, it affirms their understanding of Jesus as the Christ and Son of God and exhorts them to continue in faithful believing and living. That is, as the next chapter further demonstrates, 1 John comprises epideictic rhetoric.

6

What Genre of Writing is 1 John? Epideictic Rhetoric

In Chapter 4, I discussed the structure of 1 John by focusing on ways that its content, style, themes, and rhetorical techniques link the writing's short units together to create its address to its audience. In Chapter 5, I argued that this audience primarily comprises not opponents and secessionists, but Jesus-followers who are affirmed and instructed in being faithful in their commitment to Jesus. That is, the writing is pastoral not polemical.

In this chapter, I develop this analysis by arguing that the genre of the writing functions as an epideictic speech. It seeks to confirm and strengthen the recipients' identity as loyal adherents to Jesus.

Genre?

As noted in Chapter 1, there is little agreement or clarity about the genre of 1 John. Second and Third John exhibit the common features of a letter so 1 John, commonly associated with them, is also often referred to as a letter or epistle.

The problem, however, is that 1 John does not have common features of a letter. The opening does not identify its sender or recipients. There is no greeting ("Grace and peace …") nor thanksgiving ("I thank my God …"). And the ending does not include common features such as greetings to common acquaintances, a final wish, a closing farewell or benediction. Yet, to add some confusion, the writing *does* include one feature that is common in letters—it directly addresses its recipients with the second-person plural pronoun "you."

This second-person form of address, of course, occurs in numerous other genres. Accordingly, other genres have been suggested for 1 John such as sermons, treatises, and a "church order" or "community rule."[1]

In this chapter, I propose that 1 John functions as a written speech, specifically an epideictic speech. Epideictic rhetoric functions to strengthen the recipients' identity, praising commitments and virtues, often set over against figures who are presented as contrasts. As an epideictic speech, 1 John functions to strengthen the identity and commitments of the recipients as loyal adherents to the values and faith that they already hold, especially fellowship and life with the writer and with God and Jesus (1 Jn 1:3). The rhetoric upholds and praises these commitments and identity while contrasting them with, and attacking, commitments, identity, and practices that characterize enemies of God: false prophets, antichrists, the world.[2]

"I am Writing"

Some thirteen times the author declares his (?) purposes for writing by using an "I am writing" formula. These statements express important aspects of the identity and way of life that the speech both confirms and constructs:

- "We are writing these things so that our joy may be complete" (1 Jn 1:4). "Our joy" is defined by verse 3, which expresses the writing's central desire for fellowship between the author and the recipients, and with God and Jesus.

- "My little children, I am writing these things to you so that you may not sin" (1 Jn 2:1). To live in God's light and ways rather than in sin is the desired goal for the recipients (1 Jn 1:5-8). Yet the writing recognizes the reality of sinful behavior. The recipients have not yet attained perfection. The speech assures them that in the meantime Jesus cleanses and effects forgiveness for confessed sins (1 Jn 1:7-10).

- "Beloved, I am writing you no new commandment, but an old commandment that you have had from the beginning ... Yet I am

---

[1] Julian Hills, "A Genre for 1 John." In Birgir Pearson (ed.), *The Future of Early Christianity: Essays in Honor of Helmut Koester* (Minneapolis: Fortress, 1991), 367–77.

[2] For an analysis of features of 1 John's epideictic rhetoric, see Duane Watson, "Amplification Techniques in I John: The Interaction of Rhetorical Style and Invention," *JSNT* 51 (1993): 99–123. For an analysis of the writing's construction of identity, see Rikard Roitto, "Identity in 1 John: Sinless Sinners who Remain In Him." In J. Brian Tucker and Coleman Baker (eds), *T & T Clark Handbook to Social Identity in the New Testament* (London: T&T Clark, 2014), 493–510.

writing you a new commandment ..." (1 Jn 2:7-8). The subsequent verses (1 Jn 2:9-11) elaborate this old-new commandment as the central practice of love, not hate, for a fellow believer. The recipients are reminded of a commandment that they already know.

- "I am writing to you, little children, because your sins are forgiven" (1 Jn 2:12). The writer celebrates the forgiveness that the imperfect believers receive.

- "I am writing to you, fathers, because you know him who is from the beginning" (1 Jn 2:13a). The writer affirms their identity and experience of knowing God and/or Jesus.

- "I am writing to you, young people, because you have conquered the evil one" (1 Jn 2:13b). The speech presents the evil one, the devil, as the chief opponent of God and the recipients, and the one who inspires sin (1 Jn 3:10). The writer celebrates the believers' victory over the devil in fellowship with the divine.

- "I write to you, children, because you know the Father," and "I write to you, fathers, because you know him who is from the beginning" (1 Jn 2:14a-b). The repetition underscores the affirmation of 1 John 2:13a of their identity and experience of knowing God.

- "I write to you, young people, because you are strong and the word of God abides in you, and you have overcome the evil one" (1 Jn 2:14c). Three affirmations conclude the six "I write" statements in 2:12-14. The only use of the adjective "strong" in 1 John signifies the identity and commitment to God of the young. God's word abides in them to sustain and guide their identity and way of life. And in aligning with God, they overcome the devil.

- "I write to you, not because you do not know the truth, but because you know it ..." (1 Jn 2:21). The writer affirms the recipients' existing alignment with and commitment to the truth in contrast to the liars who deny Jesus as the Christ.

- "I write these things to you concerning those who would deceive you" (1 Jn 2:26). The writer warns the recipients against being deceived by antichrists and liars who are hostile to them and to God.

- "I write these things to you who believe in the name of the Son of God, so that you may know that you have eternal life" (1 Jn 5:13). The writer affirms two key attributes of the recipients' identity: their belief in or commitment to Jesus the Son or agent of God, and their attainment of life in the age to come ("eternal life"). The verse signifies the accomplishment of the writer's goal named in 1 John 1:2.

These "I write" statements have affirmed central attributes of the identity and commitments of the recipients: fellowship with "us" and God and Jesus; having been forgiven for sin; dedication to loving fellow believers; knowing God; victorious over the devil; pledged to the truth; warned against deceivers; belief in the Son of God; gaining "life of the age." These attributes are commended throughout the speech to emphasize their importance for the recipients' identity. First John affirms this identity and way of life that are already in place, yet there is a mandate for ongoing performance.

Moreover, these "I write" statements reveal features of the author that prevail through the writing. He asserts his authority. He addresses the recipients as "little children," thereby constructing himself with fatherly authority to exert control over them. He rejects any diversity of belief. He articulates *the* truth that focuses on Jesus's incarnation and atoning death. He claims divine vindication (1 Jn 4:6) and has no tolerance for other beliefs. He refers to any who dissent or oppose these truths with harsh language, such as calling them "children of the devil" (1 Jn 3:2) and "antichrists" and "liars" (1 Jn 2:18-22). This language expresses his dualistic worldview; people are either with him and God, or against both. The dualism privileges an in-group and shames and excludes the rest. These features will recur in the subsequent discussion.

Defining and Praising a People

In two tractates on epideictic rhetoric attributed to a third-century rhetorician,[3] Menander of Laodicea instructs speech-makers on how to praise a city or country and people.[4] He stipulates attention to three dimensions: a people's origins; their accomplishments or habits, especially of governance and skills; and their deeds and virtues. These speeches recognize and reinforce these markers of a people's identity.

For example, in writing positively about the city of Rome, Dionysius of Halicarnassus outlines his approach that embraces these three dimensions. He begins by discussing Rome's origins. "I shall in this Book show who the founders of the city were, at what periods the various groups came together

---

[3]I follow David Balch, "Two Apologetic Encomia: Dionysius on Rome and Josephus on the Jews," *Journal for the Study of Judaism* 13 (1982): 102–22.

[4]D. A. Russell and N. G Wilson, *Menander Rhetor, Edited with Translation and Commentary* (Oxford: Clarendon, 1981).

and through what turns of fortune they left their native countries." In Part 2, he moves to narrate the deeds and institutions of the Romans. "And beginning with the next Book, I shall tell of the deeds they performed immediately after the founding of the city and of the customs and institutions by virtue of which their descendants advanced to so great dominion . . ." And in Part 3, he discusses the deeds and "examples of virtue in men whose superiors, whether for piety, or for justice, or for life-long self-control, or for warlike valor, no city, either Greek or barbarian has ever produced" (*Roman Antiquities* I.5.1-3).

Moreover, as Dionysius describes and commends Rome by attending to its origins, institutions or accomplishments, and its virtuous actions, he employs the technique of contrast. He commends Rome's identity by contrasting the deficiencies of other peoples. In Part 2, Rome has "so great dominion" over other weaker peoples, and in Part 3, the examples of Roman virtuous deeds are unmatched by anything Greeks or barbarians can exhibit. Dionysius continually compares Roman customs with Greek customs to establish the superiority of the former and inferiority of the latter. Such contrasts highlight what he is commending.

A second example of the use of these three categories to define a people appears in the Jewish historian, Josephus (*Against Apion* 2.145-219).

Josephus begins by setting his construction of Jewish identity in the context of the "ignorance" and "ill will" of critics Apollonius Molon and Lysimachus who have "maligned" Moses "as a charlatan and imposter" who teaches vice and not virtue. Josephus starts with the origins of the people and the antiquity of their laws. He claims that "each nation endeavours to trace its own institutions back to the remotest date" but "our legislator [Moses] is the most ancient of all legislators in the records of the whole world" (*Ag. Ap.* 2.152, 154). All other lawgivers copied their laws from Moses (2.257, 281). Josephus narrates the people's origins from Egypt guided by Moses and God (2.157-63).

Josephus then moves from origins to "customs and laws" (2.164-70). He acknowledges three forms of government, namely monarchy, oligarchy, and rule by the masses. The Jewish constitution, however, is a theocracy in which "all sovereignty and authority" reside in God. Recognizing religion as the supreme value from which all virtues derive, Josephus moves to the people's actions and deeds, the third element of defining the identity and way of life of Jewish people (2.171-219). Moses the magnificent guides daily living to ensure societal harmony, piety, justice, and temperance. Josephus covers a wide range of virtuous actions and deeds: "education and moral training," life in the home (eating, working, resting on the Sabbath), worshipping God in the temple, marriage laws, gender relations and sexuality, upbringing of children, rituals for the dead, honor for parents, justice without bribes, protection of property, welcome for those who respect "our customs," supplying material necessities to those in need, merciful interactions, penalties for wrongdoing, the reward of a future good life.

Throughout, Josephus makes comparisons with Spartan and Greek practices. And he follows the three-dimensioned construction with a sustained contrast that rejects the criticisms of Lysimachus and Molon and asserts Jewish superiority over Spartans, Persians, and Greeks (2.296).

Josephus' account mixes description and prescription, the actual and the ideal, in constructing and narrating Jewish identity and way of life. He discusses the three areas of the people's origins, customs and laws (governance), and actions and deeds. Included in this defining of the identity and way of life of Jewish people are continual contrasts with the inferior practices of other peoples.

1 John: An Epideictic Speech

Recognizing this cultural practice that constructed a people's identity and way of life in terms of their origin, customs and governance, and actions and deeds, I suggest that 1 John utilizes this pattern to construct and affirm the identity and way of life of this community of Jesus-believers. The speech both describes identity and a way of life, even as it also prescribes or obligates recipients to actualize this identity and way of life.

Origins

1 John establishes the origins of the Jesus-community in several ways.

The phrase "from the beginning" occurs eight times. Its importance is reflected in its initial appearance in the opening clause: "that which was from the beginning." Interpreters have long debated what "beginning" is in view.

This initial use poses several interpretive issues but offers an interpretation of the phrase that can be confirmed by subsequent uses.

> We declare to you what was from the beginning, what we have heard, what we have seen with our eyes, what we have looked at and touched with our hands, concerning the word of life—
>
> (1 Jn 1:1)

One issue impacting the interpretation of the phrase concerns the sequencing of the opening three verses. Verse 1 is interrupted by verse 2; the line of thought resumes in verse 3. Further, verse 1 is the direct object of the main verb that does not appear until verse 3: "we proclaim" or "we declare." English translations such as the NRSV often relocate this verb from verse 3 to the opening of verse 1 to create a better sequence. Most challenging, verse 1 begins with a neuter pronoun ("which/that which/what was from the beginning"). But the neuter pronoun does not have an antecedent or referent. There is no eligible noun in verses 1-3 to function as the pronoun's referent. The two nouns in verses 1 and 2 are "word," which is masculine, and "life," which is feminine. There is no neuter noun for which the pronoun substitutes.

Interpreters are left, then, to supply a referent for this neuter pronoun. Suggestions abound as to what "beginning" is in view. Some suggest the beginning of all time. Some, hearing echoes of Genesis 1:1, claim the beginning of creation. Some, hearing echoes of John's Gospel 1:1, suggest Jesus as a preexistent and preincarnate being. Some argue that the unstated referent is the whole of Jesus's ministry. Some point to the first proclamation of the Gospel when the recipients of the speech first received and believed the proclamation.

Of these options, I think the last is most persuasive. 1 John does not evoke the beginning of creation, nor Adam and Eve, nor Jesus's preexistence. If the "beginning" was Jesus's ministry, the "we" of verse 1 would refer to eye-witnesses of Jesus's activity. But the (uncertain but reasonable) dating of 1 John to around 100–120 CE rules out that possibility. The verbs in verses 1-3 emphasize sensory experience and the first verb in that list is "heard." This verb suggests an experience of and appropriation of proclamation. "Proclaim" is the main verb of verse 3.

Other uses of the phrase "from the beginning" sustain this understanding that the "beginning" refers to the recipients' reception of the Gospel proclamation as the origin of the believing community. Chapter 2 verse 7 reads:

> Beloved, I am writing you no new commandment, but an old commandment that you have had from the beginning; the old commandment is the word that you have heard.

The verse introduces a section (1 Jn 2:7-11) concerning the old-new commandment to love, not hate, community members. This commandment could evoke the teaching of Lev. 19:17-18 that exhorts love for one's neighbor. Yet the plural "you" in the verb "that you have had from the beginning" suggests a common experience for all recipients of the speech, not something that some—only those familiar with the LXX—would know. More significantly, having this old-new command from the beginning is elaborated as "the word you have heard." This hearing from the beginning points to the proclamation that originated the believing community.

The exhortation of 1 John 2:24 reinforces this reference to their embracing of the founding proclamation.

> Let what you heard from the beginning abide in you. If what you heard from the beginning abides in you, then you will abide in the Son and in the Father.

The twofold reference to "from the beginning" occurs in relation to "what they have heard." It signifies a determinative and initial experience of hearing the preached Gospel that constructs their identity and way of life. Further, if "what you heard" abides in them, it creates what the rest of the sentence names as the relationship or "fellowship" with the Son and the Father. Loyalty to the Son and the Father is constituent of the community, a fundamental item of the proclamation that the hearers have embraced in the origin of the community (1 Jn 2:24b; 5:10, 13, 20). The verb "abide" is a marker of having received the proclamation, fellowship with the Father and Son, and the obligation to live accordingly (1 Jn 2:6; 3:9).

The same definition of "the beginning" as the recipients' origin in receiving the initial proclamation is evident in 1 John 3:11 with its statement of the ongoing obligation to love.

> For this is the message you have heard from the beginning, that we should love one another.

Again the verb "hearing" is associated with the phrase "from the beginning." And the noun "message" emphasizes the proclamation whose reception marks the origin of the believing community. The proclamation declares an ongoing obligation to love other members of the community.

Two remaining uses repeat the same point.

> I am writing to you, fathers, because you know him who is from the beginning . . . I write to you, fathers, because you know him who is from the beginning.

> (1 Jn 2:13a, 14b)

Consistent with the emphasis on the proclamation that founded the community, these two verses do not make an abstract theological and/or Christological statement that God and Jesus existed in the beginning of time. Rather, the three references to God as father in verses 15-17 suggest a theocentric reference whereby God was revealed to community members in the initial proclamation.

But further, I suggest Jesus is also in view as one known "from the beginning" in the initial community-establishing proclamation. That proclamation concerned fellowship with God as Father and with Jesus as Son (1 Jn 1:3). To deny or reject the Son is to deny or reject the Father; to "confess the Son [is to have] the Father also" (2:22-4). The initial proclamation made knowing God and Jesus possible. "If what you heard from the beginning abides in you, then you will abide in the Son and in the Father . . . [which is] eternal life" (1 Jn 2:24; cf. 4:15). The perfect tense of the verb "know" indicates a past experience of knowing with continuing implications for the present. The origin of the Jesus-community lies in receiving the message at the outset which enables knowing both God and Jesus. The writer assumes the role of authenticating the recipients' foundational and normative belief.

One other beginning should be noted. This beginning disrupts relationship with God. In 1 Jn 3:8, the "beginning" refers to the devil's sinning:

> Everyone who commits sin is a child of the devil; for the devil has been sinning from the beginning. The Son of God was revealed for this purpose, to destroy the works of the devil.

The devil sins "from the beginning" and people sin too. The designation "child of the devil" suggests the devil as the cause of people sinning. Verse 12 constructs Cain as coming "from the evil one" and the one who "murdered his brother" Abel (Gen. 4:1-16). Perhaps the writer suggests that this event, not Adam and Eve, began the devil's work of inspiring human sin. Or perhaps, since the verb translated as "has been sinning" is a present tense ("is sinning;" "continually sins"), it signifies that the devil always and still sins, thereby causing people to hate or not love one's brother or sister (1 Jn 3:15). Verse 8, though, subjugates the devil to the Son of God, who destroys the devil's works. Whether this destroying happens in the present, whereby the Son of God Jesus helps people not to sin, or whether the destroying is eschatological in that Jesus finally and fully destroys the devil and its actions, is unclear.

Born of God

Beyond the phrase "from the beginning," the speech refers to the recipients' origins in other ways.

Six times the speech employs an image of birth to affirm the recipients' origin as "born of God." The image highlights the divine work of bringing this community of Jesus-followers into being. In 1 John 3:9, father God's seed or sperm generates their new life and identity. This is the community's origin whether by means of the proclaimed word which they have heard or the action of the Spirit (1 Jn 2:20, 27; Ezek. 36:26-7; John 3:3, 5). Yet verse 9 also maintains that not only does this sperm originate the addressees, but it also abides or remains in these descendants and shapes lives not marked by sin.

Another expression of origin focuses on God's gifts to the recipients. In being born of God, they have passed from death to life (3:14). This eternal life—or life of the age—is God's gift in sending God's son into the world so that "we live through him" (4:9; 5:11-13). God has also given the Spirit to God's children (3:24; 4:2, 13). And their origin resides in God's love (4:16a), which creates their identity as "beloved" (2:7; 3:2, 21; 4:1, 7, 11). The writer emphasizes their privileged identity as insiders in contrast to excluded outsiders.

From/Out Of

Also expressing their origin is the preposition *ek*, which means "from" or "out of." The recipients are said to be "from God" (4:4, 6 [2x]) and "from truth" (3:19). To not do justice and to not love one's brother and sister is to show that a person is not from God (2:16). Lies are not from truth (2:21). Other forces—the world (2:16; 4:5), the devil (3:8, 12), antichrists (2:19), false prophets (4:1)—originate actions and pressures that threaten the believing community and oppose God.

The speech emphasizes in multiple ways the recipients' origins. They have heard and received the initial proclamation about God's dealings in God's son Jesus. Being born of God constitutes their identity in fellowship with God and Jesus. They are differentiated from "children of the devil," children who originate from the devil; children born of God do justice and love brothers and sisters (3:10). This binary serves to privilege the recipients while rejecting any diversity or departure from the writer's "normalizing" beliefs.

Habits of Governance and Laws

The second aspect of the three-part pattern for defining and describing a people concerns their forms of governance and laws.

First John does not recognize an established hierarchy of community leaders. Nor does it expose and critique incompetent and narcissistic leadership that lords it over and disrespects community members. Rather, the speech entrusts the community as a whole with tasks of governance.

One governance responsibility concerns discerning those who truly belong to the community. Several criteria exist for this discernment. One criterion involves confessions concerning Jesus: that Jesus is the Christ (2:22) who has come in the flesh (4:2), "believing in the name of his Son Jesus Christ" (3:23), confessing that Jesus is the Son of God (4:15) which means having the Father (2:23b). Since this Christological confession is so integral to community membership, perhaps the confession was public, audible, visible, communal, and accountable to others. Failure to confess would result in either remediation or exclusion.

A second criterion for discerning who truly belongs to the community involves attitudes and practices concerning sin. The noun "sin" occurs seventeen times and the verb "sin" ten times in 1 John. On one hand, recipients are exhorted not to sin since sinning derives from the devil (3:8-9). More nuanced, they are at least to adopt a perfectionist goal of sinlessness (2:1a; 2:3; 3:6, 9; 5:18). Yet on the other hand, their imperfection or committing of sin is not to be denied (1:8, 10). Sin is to be confessed (1:9a) knowing that Jesus's death as an atoning sacrifice (2:1-2) offers forgiveness (1:9; 2:12; 3:4-5).

How is this practice of confession and forgiveness monitored? The emphasis on accountability again suggests public confession. Just as public confession of Jesus's identity is central to group membership, so might public confession of sin express a person's commitment to the group's value of resisting sin. Forgiveness, then, is conferred presumably through and with other community members. Extending forgiveness restores relationships not only with God but with community members, signifying a relational restoration or integration as a brother or sister who embraces communal values, and preventing punitive or vengeful acts. And, it perhaps follows that there might be communal action (remediation? exclusion?) for those who refuse to acknowledge or confess their sins.[5]

Near its end, the speech confirms and addresses this matter of relational or communal accountability. Members are to discern and address a brother or sister "sinning a sin not to death" (5:16a, "not a mortal sin"), but they are not to bother with the sin that is "to death" (5:16b, "mortal"). Sin is assumed to be public. The community is assumed not only to be aware of it but also

---

[5]Informing this section is Rikard Roitto, "Practices of Confession, Intercession, and Forgiveness in 1 John 1:9; 5:16." *NTS* 58 (2012): 235–53, though I reject his attempt at mirror-reading 1 John 1:8–10 (247–8).

to be able to distinguish the difference between mortal and not-mortal sin. Then it is to take appropriate action concerning not-mortal sins. This action involves praying for the sinner with the assurance that "God will give life to such a one" (5:16).

This prayer would seek the member to repent and halt their sinful action. With public/communal confession, public/communal forgiveness follows with reconciliation with the victim (when the offense is against a brother or sister). How is life, in the form of communal restoration, to be mediated? Most likely it seems that it is arbitrated by community members whose involvement seeks the restoration rather than the punishment of the person.

The speech instructs that prayer is not to be offered for sins that are "to death." These "mortal" sins would comprise behaviors that signify a person is not a genuine community member: refusing or denying Christological confession; not confessing sin; not loving community brothers and sisters (see pp. 96–97). Those who persistently sin in these ways are not born of God (5:18). Such behaviors deviate profoundly from the identity and way of life that the speech is constructing and affirming. These sinners cannot "remain" in the community. They go out "from us" (1 Jn 2:19).

A third criterion for discerning true community members concerns the command to love the brothers and sisters. The repetition of this command emphasizes it to show the importance of this verifiable action for the identity of community members (3:16; 4:7, 8, 11, 12, 19, 20, 21). Loving one another derives from God loving "us so much" (4:11). When community members love one another, "God lives in us" (4:12). To love God mandates love for brothers and sisters (4:21).

As with confessions of Christology and sin, loving brothers and sisters is a public and visible test of community membership. Sharing or not sharing one's goods with a brother or sister in need is a very practical and visible demonstration of whether God's love abides in a person or not (3:16-17). Love is to be expressed "in truth and action" (3:18). Similarly, hating a brother or sister would be revealed in actions and manifests one to be a "liar" (4:20). Moreover, not doing justice and not loving one's brothers and sisters—both visible and public acts—reveals one to be a child of the devil (3:10).

The speech entrusts community governance not to a group of leaders but to everyone belonging to it. Community members monitor each other's performance of identity markers of Christological confession, acknowledgment of sin even as one aspires to perfection, and love for each other. These markers require public and visible actions that demonstrate a person's genuine membership. The absence of compliance presumably results in either remediation or departure/expulsion.

Deeds and Virtuous Actions

The discussion has identified some deeds and actions that 1 John affirms as constituent of the identity and way of life of community members. Their identity is praxis-driven. These public and visible actions include doing justice (2:29), not sinning (3:9), loving members of the Jesus-community (4:7), believing Jesus is the Christ (5:1), conquering the world (5:4), not sinning and protecting others from the evil one (5:18). Predictably, the recipients are addressed as "children" whom God loves (3:1) and who experience eschatological realities now (2:18) and in the future (3:2).

Three further actions are identified.

The first of these affirms and exhorts "keeping and doing the commandments" (2:3-6; 3:22-4; 5:2-3). Obeying the commandments denotes abiding in Jesus (3:24). The speech does not list specific commands to be obeyed, however, with the exception of practical love for members who lack "the world's goods," in the sense of being economically disavantaged (3:11, 17; 4:21). Perhaps we can posit that central requirements in the biblical tradition for ethical living are in view, such as the Decalogue (Exod. 20:1-21). Murder, one of the Decalogue's commandments, is forbidden in 1 Jn 3:15.

Also to be noted is the threefold use of the noun to designate the recipients' doing of "justice" (*dikaiosunē*; 1 Jn 2:29; 3:7, 10) or "doing what is right." This latter translation masks the term's long-standing referent for God's justice-doing work in delivering the oppressed and setting injustice right (Isa. 51:5-6). When the king does "righteousness" or "justice" in Psalm 72, he acts faithfully to the covenant in defending the poor, delivering the needy, crushing the oppressor, and exercising life-giving dominion over the earth. If this biblical tradition is in view, the recipients have the task of manifesting God's justice as an alternative community in the midst of the Roman empire in which injustice in the form of elite privilege and domination is pervasive. Central to this obedience and doing justice is "doing the will of God" (2:17) and "doing what pleases him" (4:22b).

Second, the speech expresses an expectation that community members love God. This love for God is constructed first as a response to the expression of God's love in sending Jesus to atone for sins (4:10-11a). And love for God is expressed in loving those who belong to the community (4:11b). To declare love for God yet to hate community members rather than assist them reveals a person to be a liar who is unable to love the invisible God (4:20-1). Love for God is also expressed in obeying the commandments (5:2-3a). The speech does not explicitly link love for God with acts of worship, though praying for a sinful member and mediating forgiveness could be construed as an act of love not only for that person but also for God (cf. 5:14-17).

Third, the speech identifies some actions that are *not* to be taken. A direct command forbids "love for the world" (2:15). The world does not designate creation. Rather, verse 15 sets the world in antithesis to God. Those who love the world do not know the "love of the Father." This antithesis suggests that "the world" refers to anything and anyone that resists divine purposes and will. Love for the world is another indicator that a community member does not belong. Again the writer employs a binary to delineate the favored ingroup and the shamed and excluded outgroup.

Throughout, the world is constructed negatively. It is associated with sin (2:2), with not knowing God (3:1), with hate for community members (3:13). It is the domain of false prophets (4:1) and antichrists (4:3). It "lies under the power of the evil one" (5:19). Yet this realm of people and its societal structures, deemed to be opposed to God, is not irredeemable. God seeks its salvation by sending God's son into the world to save from sins and to give life as the imperially imitative savior of the world (2:2; 4:9, 14). But the world seems resistant to the divine purposes (4:5). Despite the world's hateful opposition to community members (3:13), the community lives in its midst: "so are we in the world" (4:17). The speech provides assurance that community members, though hated, are born of God and so "conquer the world" through faith. It is unclear whether this victory comes through "faith" that consists of "believing that Jesus is the Son of God" (5:5) or through faithfulness demonstrated in their way of life.

Yet despite the assurance of victory the speech also warns that "the world" threatens community members (2:15-17). Verse 16 identifies its threats or allures with a threefold phrase: "the desire of the flesh, the desire of the eyes, the pride in riches" (NRSV).

The meaning of the three terms is unclear. Some have sought specific identifiers for each term; for example, sex, covetousness, wealth; or honors, riches, pleasures. Others have settled on a general description of anything that seductively lures believers away from faithfulness to God. Given the negative association of the term "world," the "desires" for "all that is in the world" and of "the flesh and eyes" warn against and disapprove of seeking for anything not found in life lived in fellowship with Father and the Son.

The third item is especially difficult given the ambiguity of the language reflected in translations such as "the arrogance of life" or "the pride in riches" (NRSV). Perhaps the phrase warns against a quest for material possessions in a context in which some 70–80 percent of the population experienced degrees of poverty. Or perhaps it warns against boasting in or holding close one's resources when other community members have unmet needs (3:17). Or perhaps it critiques arrogant self-confidence that seeks to define and secure one's life apart from trust in God.

The writing constructs the "world" as a threatening and dangerous place for those addressed by the writing, yet the verses warn that its allure is not simply "out there." It is present in, available to, and seductive among community members who are warned not to be diverted or attracted by the world's commitments and practices. Community members are assured, however, that the world is passing away (2:17). The eschatological perspective reinforces the divide between God and the oppositional world, as well as emphasizing that the world poses a threat that is, nevertheless, temporary, limited, and subjected to the divine purposes with which the community is aligned.

Conclusion

The rhetoric of this epideictic speech affirms the community members' origin, governance, and actions. It sustains a dualism or contrast that is fundamental to their identity and way of life. They are of God and not of the world (4:4-6). As doers of God's will they remain forever, unlike those who love the world that passes away (2:17). They are children of God, not children of the devil (3:8-10). They know life of the age while others know death (3:14-15). They have the Father and the Son in contrast to those who do not (2:23; 5:12). They have the Spirit of God and not the "spirit of the antichrist" (4:2-3). They belong to truth and not falsehood or lies (1:6; 2:4, 21; 4:6).

This identity shapes a communal way of life marked by Christological confession, seeking to live a sin-free life while also confessing sin and receiving forgiveness, love for community members, obeying commandments, knowing and loving God, doing justice, resisting the world's threat, and living life. As an epideictic speech, 1 John affirms and constructs this identity and way of life.

Evaluation

What are the strengths and weaknesses of the identity and commitments that 1 John as an epideictic speech affirms and encourages?

The speech outlines and exhorts, describes and prescribes, informs and forms a strong identity and concomitant way of life. Beginning with acceptance of the proclamation in confessing Christ, being "born of God," and coming "from God" and "from truth," community members have received the Spirit and God's love, and they know God and life of the age. Now they are constructed as being obligated to live in accountability to one another, to strive for sinless perfection yet to confess their sins, to obey the commandments, and, especially, to love one another. This identity and way of life are lived in the context of, and surrounded and resisted by, opposing realities: the world, antichrists, false prophets, liars. The devil inspires such opposing forces. The speech constructs a binary of insiders and outsiders, children of God and children of the devil.

With this binary, the writer assumes the position of neatly—and viciously—dividing those of God from those of the devil to construct a tidy, even comforting, worldview for insiders. Yet the binary is deceptive because human life is never this neat and simple. Ambivalences in the speech—sinless perfection yet confessing sin, loving community members yet hating them—reflect some awareness of complexities that might threaten the binary yet it is able to subsume the threat. The sins of community members can be forgiven; God's love ensures love for community members. The binary remains in place,

The binary also sanctions the community's intolerance of and disregard for outsiders. While the speech admits that Jesus's atoning sacrifice is "also for the sins of the whole world" (1 Jn 2:2), there is no attention to breeching the binary to proclaim this atoning sacrifice and the forgiveness of sins to outsiders. The world remains a sinful, hostile, threatening, untouchable, unreceptive entity under the power of the devil (1 Jn 5:19). It is a place of temptation (1 Jn 2:16). It is not the object of the community's mission. God might love the world and "send his only Son into the world" as its savior (1 Jn 4:9, 14) but the community does not love the world and is not sent in mission to it. The community's love extends only to brothers and sister. The community can be comforted by knowing that inevitably the world does not listen to "us" and listens only to itself (1 Jn 4:5-6) so there's no point trying. And anyway, "the world and its desires are passing away" (1 Jn 2:17). The world is a "fixed" oppositional entity providing a "fixed" point in a rigid binary—until it passes away in eschatological judgment. To write off most of human community and culture in this way is arrogant, demeaning, and tragic.

There is also a theological deception. The writer's binary allies God with the insiders. God is very much the possession of "us.". "We" have experienced God's love (1 Jn 4:16a). "We" are the "beloved" (1 Jn 2:7 etc.). "We" are the ones who know God and have fellowship with God and Jesus (1 Jn 1:3). God answers "our" prayers (1 Jn 5:16). God's love is absent from "those who love the world" (1 Jn 2:15). God abides with those who confess Jesus as the Son of God (1 Jn 4:15) not with those who do not confess. Starting with the creation story in Genesis 1, numerous Hebrew Bible traditions affirm God's concern for the well-being of all of creation. The binary of 1 John, though, does not embrace this affirmation and understanding of God. It excludes most of human culture and society from the loving purposes of God.

True to epideictic rhetoric, 1 John constructs and conforms a strong and clear identity and way of life for its addressees. Yet there is fallout from the construction. The writer's binary does not value human life outside the community of believers. It rejects diversity, is intolerant of dissenters, shames and excludes those deemed to be opponents, and constructs God as being concerned with, experienced by, and active amongst only the privileged community of believers.

7

Theology in 1 John

In Chapter 6, I argued that 1 John is an epideictic speech that affirms and constructs the identity and way of life of its recipients. It does so by addressing their origin, customs and governance, and actions and deeds as Jesus-believers. In this chapter, I identify the theological claims that 1 John makes that contribute to this identity-constructing and affirming work.

To be clear, I am not suggesting that 1 John is primarily a theological treatise. It does not include content just to check off common theological claims. As an epideictic speech, its theological claims function to inform, sustain, and reinforce the identity and lifestyle of the recipients as Jesus-believers that the speech constructs and sustains. The theology is pastoral, functional, identity-constituting, much more than dogmatic, propositional, systematic.

I start with its presentation of God, the originator of the community, then believing in Jesus as God's agent, before moving on to ecclesial life with its love for brothers and sisters, the Spirit, and eschatological goal. Since these theological claims are in the service of the speech's identity-forming function, there will be some overlap with Chapter 6.

God

The speech's references to God are not abstract statements. God is not distant and remote, a vague, impersonal force in the cosmos. Rather, 1 John constructs God as closely involved with Jesus and the community of Jesus-followers.

As Father (1 Jn 1:2-3; 2:1, 14-16, 22-4; 3:1; 4:14), God brings believers into being. God supplies seed that not only produces believers but can also produce their sinless life (1 Jn 1:2; 3:9). And in an instance of gender-bending, God, though a Father, also gives birth to community members as a mother. They are born of God (1 Jn 2:29; 3:9; 4:7; 5:1, 4, 18) and are from God (1 Jn 4:4, 6). This divine activity creates their identity as God's children (1 Jn 3:1-2a).

> See what love the Father has given us, that we should be called children of God; and that is what we are . . . Beloved, we are God's children now.

This birthing activity also expresses God's identity as love (1 Jn 4:8, 16). Divine love is not a feeling, but rather an action that creates community members as "beloved" (1 Jn 2:7; 3:2, 21; 4:1, 7, 11). God reveals God's love through sending Jesus to deal with "our" sins along with "the sins of the whole world," to be the "savior of the world," to provide ongoing life (1 Jn 2:2; 4:9-10, 14). God loves and thereby equips community members to obey God's commandments (5:2-3) and carry out their distinctive practice of love for one another (1 Jn 3:1; 4:7, 10-11, 16, 21).

> We love because he first loved us.
>
> (1 Jn 4:19)

God is also light (1 Jn 1:5). Again this description does not construct God as distant, mystical, and elusive, but as active in constructing the identity of community members. As light, God enables fellowship with God and ethical relational living with other community members (1 Jn 1:3-7). Knowing God as light means living in fellowship with God and cleansed of sin (1:6-7). It means not living in darkness which denies God's presence and purposes. It means not hating another believer (2:9-11).

Further, God gives the life that constitutes the present and future identity of the believing community (1 Jn 1:1-2). This divine action identifies believers as having passed from death to life (3:14). With God is "life of the age" (1:2), which is a gift to community members through Jesus in the present and future (2:25; 5:11, 20). Even sinful members know this life (5:16). God "lives" and "abides in" community members who in turn make God visible and present (3:24; 4:12, 16). Community members live in (2:5b) and abide in God (2:24, 27-8; 4:15). This life of the age is eschatological known in fullness with Jesus's return (3:2).

First John also names God as righteous or just. And again this characteristic denotes God's actions. God's justice-doing activity, paired with God's faithfulness, constitutes the community of believers as a community forgiven of and cleansed from confessed sin (1:9). The verse indicates that God does the right thing in response to confession of sin. If 2:29 refers to God, God's actions for justice are generalized and reflected in the justice-doing actions of members of the believing community (3:7, 17). The doing or not doing of justice divides God's children from those who are children of the devil who fail to do justice (3:7-8).

This "up-close-and-personal" God is known in the believing community (1 Jn 4:7). God answers prayers and supplies "whatever we ask" (1 Jn 3:22; 5:15). God "hears us" (1 Jn 5:14-15). God gives commandments for community members to follow and to do God's will (1 Jn 2:17; 4:21). The God of 1 John is a Father who is love, light, life-giving, just, active, present, in whom Jesus and believers abide (1 Jn 2:5-6; 2:24, 27-8; 3:24; 4:12-16; 5:20). These qualities denote God in action, oriented to the believing community, constructing its identity and lifestyle. Consistent with the writer's intolerance of diversity, disqualification of pluralist identities, and binary worldview, 1 John's God is not especially generous to the nonbelieving world, even though God sent Jesus into the world to reveal God's love (1 Jn 4.9) and to effect forgiveness "for the sins of the whole world" (1 Jn 2:2).

Believing in Jesus

The identity of the addressees as "born of God" and being "from God" might suggest that God pre-selects some people to become God's children. Two factors modify this view.

One is a matter of perspective. The claim to be God's children and to be from God is made "looking back." It reviews previous experience concerning those who have become members of the Jesus-community by believing the proclamation they heard "in the beginning." It affirms the privileged identity of these insiders.

The second factor involves the members' commitment to Jesus and to God denoted by the language of "believing." Basic to believing is understanding Jesus as the son or agent of God's saving presence in the world which has reconciled the recipients with Jesus and God. Again it is not primarily a matter of checking off doctrinal affirmations but constructing the identity and way of life of the recipients.

Believing or confessing Jesus involves three dimensions (1 Jn 4:3). One is to recognize that Jesus is from God and is an agent or representative of God. The second involves loyalty to Jesus rather than opposition as an "antichrist" (1 Jn 4:3b). The third is to be obedient by loving community members.

Jesus is identified as the "Christ" (1 Jn 1:3; 2:1, 22; 3:23; 4:2; 5:1, 6, 20). The term "Christ" literally means "anointed" or "sanctioned for" or "appointed to" a particular role in divine service. In the Hebrew Bible, it designates priests anointed for temple service (Lev. 4:3, 5 etc.), prophets anointed to speak God's will to circumstances of power and injustice (1 Kgs 19:16), kings anointed to represent God's rule among the people (e.g. Pss. 2:2; 72), and the Persian ruler Cyrus who is anointed to set free Jewish exiles in Babylon and to return them to their land (Isa. 44:28; 45:1). To call Jesus "Christ" is to locate him with those who are "anointed" to represent divine purposes.

What purposes does Jesus represent? The first reference associates Jesus with fellowship with God and the authors (1 Jn 1:3). This fellowship is created through the proclaimed word that reveals life (1 Jn 1:2). This link suggests that the proclamation concerned Jesus as a revealer of God's life and purposes. The Christological statement functions to constitute the blessed and privileged identity of the speech's recipients and to divide them from non-believers.

Moreover, in another identity-forming statement, Jesus Christ is an "advocate" (*paraklēton*) with the Father (1 Jn 2:1). In John's Gospel, this term referred several times to the Spirit's ministry with believers in their daily, earthly lives (John 14:16, 26; 15:26; 16:7); here it refers to Jesus in heaven in God's presence. What is Jesus's role? The Hebrew Bible attests those who intercede with God for others such as Abraham interceding for Sodom (Gen. 18:2-33) and Moses interceding for Pharaoh (Exod. 8:28-9). More analogous are intercessors in the heavens such as those sought by Job (Job 16:19-22) or envisioned in Zechariah 3 with Joshua as high priest in the heavenly court. In this tradition, Jesus is understood to be in heaven praying before God for believers.

Yet also, an adversary, Satan, is present in the heavenly court to make accusations against people before God (Job 2; Zech. 3). The Satan, for example, accuses Job of being fickle in his allegiance to God and challenges God to expose Job. In this tradition, Jesus's role is to defend believers before God. This role would be consistent with 1 John 3:8 that recognizes that as God's son Jesus has destroyed the works of the devil. Taking the two traditions together, Jesus has a double role in the heavens, to make intercession for believers and to be an advocate defending accused believers.

A further important term follows in 1 John 2:2. Jesus Christ is a *hilasmos* for sins (also 1 Jn 4:10). The term is variously translated to identify Jesus as "the means of atonement" or "the atoning sacrifice" (NRSV) or the "expiation" or the "atoning action" or "the forgiveness for our sins." Some claim Jesus's death is a sacrificial act and appeal to the day of atonement ritual in Leviticus 16. But Leviticus 16 does not use this word. In fact, the uses of this word in the Septuagint (the Greek translation of the Hebrew Bible) are more frequently non-cultic and simply refer generically to "forgiveness" (Ps. 130:4 [LXX129:4]; Dan. 9:9; Sir. 18:20; 35:5 = to forsake injustice).[1] In this context, the term identifies Jesus as forgiveness or the means of forgiveness "for our sins." The emphasis is on the accomplishment of forgiveness rather than on the means by which he accomplishes this task.

Commitment to Jesus as Christ is central to the identity and way of life of the believing community (1 Jn 2:22). This commitment means recognizing Jesus as the Christ, the one whom God has anointed or sanctioned. This confession separates the believing community from antichrists who deny God and Jesus (2:22b; 4:3). To "believe that Jesus is the Christ" constitutes the identity of the believing community as being born of God (1 Jn 5:1). So community members have "believed in the name of Jesus Christ" which mandates the practice of love for other community members (1 Jn 3:23). They have believed that Jesus Christ "has come in the flesh" and is "from God" (1 Jn 4:2). The confession affirms Jesus's revelatory activity in his incarnational ministry (1 Jn 5:6) and the source of its legitimacy: he is from God. God testifies to Jesus (1 Jn 5:9-10). Believers live in him (5:20). The speech presents Jesus Christ in his roles in relation to the community's identity and way of life.

Jesus is also identified as "Son" or "Son of God" some twenty-two times.[2] This term also underscores his role as agent of the divine purposes that shape the recipients' identity.

Across the Hebrew Bible, the term recognizes close relationship with God and a special identity and task. Kings, for example, are a son or child of God (Ps. 2:7) in close relationship with God and entrusted with representing God's rule. Israel is God's son or child in covenant relationship with God and entrusted with being obedient and a light to the nations (Hos. 11:1).

In 1 John, as Son/Son of God, Jesus is in close relationship with God as agent of God's purposes. The term "Son" is used in association with fellowship or abiding among believers, Jesus and God (1 Jn 1:3; 2:23-4; 4:15). The antichrists deny the relationship between "the Father and the Son" that

---

[1] To complete the listings, Lev. 25:9 discusses the sabbatical year and makes a very general passing reference to the day of atonement for dating purposes; Num. 5:8, an offering when someone wrongs a neighbor and seeks forgiveness; 2 Macc. 3:32-3, an offering for Heliodorus' healing.
[2] 1 John 1:3, 7; 2:22, 23 [2x], 24; 3:8, 23; 4:9, 10, 14, 15; 5:5, 9, 10 [2x], 11, 12 [2x], 13, 20 [2x].

sanctions Jesus's roles (2:22-23a). As son, Jesus cleanses recipients from sin (1:7; 4:10). As son, Jesus destroys the works of the devil (3:8). He reveals God and provides believers with life (4:9; 5:11-13). God sent Jesus as son or agent into the world to reveal God and manifest God's love, to provide life, to effect forgiveness for sins, and to be the savior of the world (4:9-10, 14). He displays love in laying down his love "for us" and as a model for brothers and sisters to imitate in behavior toward each other (3:16). God bears witness to or attests Jesus as son (5:9-10) and Jesus reveals God what is true (5:20).

To believe that "Jesus is the Son (agent) of God" (3:23) enables recipients to conquer the hostile world (5:5). Believing "in the Son of God" means accepting God's testimony that Jesus is God's agent and as a result encountering life of the age (5:10-11, 13). The verb "believing" is also directed toward God in believing "the love that God has for us" which constitutes their identity as "beloved" (4:16).

The verb "confess" has a similar function. Confession is not primarily cerebral affirmation but a means of relational commitment to and interaction with Jesus and God. Confessing sins means encountering God as just, faithful, and forgiving (1:9). Confessing the Son means "having" or encountering God as Father (2:23). The identifying marker of a Spirit from God is that the Spirit confesses Jesus has come in the flesh. This confession distinguishes a spirit and believer from antichrists (4:2-3). Jesus the Son identifies those who deny his identity as outsiders (2:22-3; 4:3; 5:10). While Jesus enacts God's purposes to save the world as the dominating and powerful "savior of the world" (4:14), 1 John presents human beings as generally rejecting of God and Jesus, in contrast to the believing community (3:1, 13).

The presentation of Jesus emphasizes his beneficial roles in shaping the identity and way of life of the recipients.

Ecclesiology: Abiding with God and Jesus

Perhaps 1 John's central metaphor for the identity and way of life of the believing community is "abiding." The frequent use of the verb *menō*, appearing twenty-four times in the five chapters, underscores its importance. The verb has both mystical and ethical dimensions.

Believers and God abide in each other in loving relationship (4:12, 13, 15, 16b). Believers who obey Jesus's commandments abide in him and he in them (3:24). Believers also abide in the Father and the Son and thereby receive life of the age (2:24-5). God abides in those who confess Jesus (4:15). The word of God (2:14d), anointing and teaching (2:27), and the Spirit (3:24; 4:13) abide in believers.

Beyond this mystical dimension, abiding has ethical dimensions. To claim to abide in him requires walking or living as Jesus lived (2:6). Fundamentally, this means loving the brothers and sisters (2:10; 3:14, 15, 17; 4:12). It also involves overcoming the evil one (2:14), maintaining fellowship with other believers (2:19), and not sinning (3:6, 9). Doing the will of God means abiding into the age to come at Jesus's *parousia* (2:17, 28).

And Abiding With the Spirit

The speech's references to the Spirit are not numerous but they reinforce central features of the believing community's identity and way of life. While there is no reference to a Pentecost-like event, Jesus and/or God give the Spirit to the believing community as an expression of their abiding presence (1 Jn 3:24; 4:13). It creates a binary. The God-given Spirit inspires the confession that "Jesus Christ has come in the flesh" and contrasts with the denying and oppositional spirits of the antichrist (1 Jn 4:2-3). This role in reinforcing the division between believers and non-believers arises from the alignment of God's spirit with truth while the antichrists' spirit aligns with error and the world (1 Jn 4:6). The Spirit bears witness to Jesus in his baptism (revealed as God's son and given the Spirit) and in his death as a means of forgiving sins (1 Jn 5:6, 8). Presumably these claims were part of the proclamation that the community received and believed from the beginning (1 Jn 1:1-3).

Striving for Perfection—Knowing Forgiveness

In the last chapter, I highlighted 1 John's frequent attention to sin so I will not repeat the full discussion here. Yet it is important to note that the reality of sin plays an important part in the construction of the believing community's identity and way of life.

On one hand, the speech holds out as a goal that "you may not sin" (1 Jn 2:1). To abide in "him" (God? Jesus? Both?) means not to sin; sinning indicates not seeing nor knowing God/Jesus (1 Jn 3:6; 5:18). To be born of God means not only not to "do sin" but also not to be able to sin (1 Jn 3:9). Sinning indicates alignment with the devil (1 Jn 3:8-10) but the community members have conquered the evil one (1 Jn 2:13b). Throughout, community members are exhorted and expected to obey the commandments in which love is perfected (1 Jn 2:3-5; 3:23-4; 5:2-3), to do justice and to love other community members (1 Jn 3:10).

On the other hand, however, despite the goal of sinlessness as a community marker, the speech recognizes the reality of sin. It characterizes the whole world (1 Jn 2:2) which is "under the power of the evil one" (1 Jn 5:19). Its presence among the recipients cannot be denied. To deny sin's presence is self-deception and to make God a liar (since God deems humans to be sinners? 1 Jn 1:8-10). Sin is "lawlessness," a reference perhaps to disobeying the commandments (1 Jn 3:22-4; 4:21), or failing to love the brothers and sisters (1 Jn 2:11; 3:14-17; 4:20), or to the failure to do justice (1 Jn 3:7) or the failure to confess Jesus's identity (1 Jn 3:23). Sin is forgivable through Jesus's death (1 Jn 1:7, 9; 2:2, 12; 3:5; 4:10), through the just or righteous nature of God/Jesus (1 Jn 1:9; 2:1, 29) and through a communal ritual of prayer, confession and forgiveness (1 Jn 5:14-17).

The speech does not reconcile these two strands. The affirmation of sinlessness and the recognition of the reality of sin coexist as part of the recipients' identity.

Doing Justice and Love

Consistently, 1 John is concerned with providing indicators or criteria by which members of the believing community can be recognized, by which other believers can recognize the authenticity of their lives, and by which outsiders or nonbelievers can be identified. Believing in Jesus and loving one's brothers and sisters are two commonly repeated identity markers (1 Jn 3:23). Verse 29 of Chapter 2 adds doing justice as evidence for being born of God. This praxis creates a binary and contrasts with those in 1 John 3:4 who sin and do lawlessness. Since doing justice attests being born of God, the justice performed by the community of believers must reflect the justice that God performs. Verse 7 of Chapter 3 makes the same point: "Everyone who does justice is just/righteous, just as he is just." God's righteous acts provide the model and inspiration for the acts of community members. Failing to do justice signifies a person is not from God but from the devil (1 Jn 3:10).

Cain, who murdered his brother Abel, is such a one (1 Jn 3:12, evoking Gen. 4:1-16).

And what justice does God perform? For the prophets, God enacts covenant commitments to save and judge (Isa. 42:6-7; 51:4-6). God pursues a societal vision to protect and care for the poor and needy, as well as to destroy oppressors. The royal Psalm 72, for example, begins by praying for God to "give the king your justice." This justice defends the poor, delivers the needy, and crushes oppressors (Ps 72:2-4, 12-14). The closest that 1 John comes to specifying the praxis of justice required of the community of believers in imitation of God's justice-doing work appears in 1 John 3:17-18:

> How does God's love abide in anyone who has the world's goods and sees a brother or sister in need and yet refuses help? Little children, let us love, not in word or speech, but in truth and action.

Practical care for other community members—here in the form of shared resources with those in need—provides an example of justice-doing work and of obeying the commandments. But it remains unclear as to whether the speech envisions any such actions directed toward those outside the community who lived in the Roman empire. Some 70 to 80 or so percent of the empire's population experienced gradations of poverty and struggled at various levels for survival on a daily basis with limited resources in a very hierarchical world that benefitted a small fraction of elites at the expense of the rest. Does the community of believers have any mission to this imperial world? First John does not explicitly require any such actions.

This command to express love for brothers and sisters in need links the doing of justice with the speech's repeated command to love other members of the community, the brothers and sisters. I have outlined this demand in the previous chapter also as one of the criteria for attesting that one is living the identity and way of life of a community member faithfully. This love originates with God and embodies God's love (1 Jn 4:11-12).

Opposed by Hostile Powers

The writer posits that recipients of the speech, members of the believing community, live their identity and way of life in a hostile context. In addition to their ongoing struggle with sin, he identifies numerous oppositional and binary entities, some of which I identified in the last chapter.

One such entity is "the world." It hates the believing community (1 Jn 3:13). It exists in alliance with the devil, the arch-opponent of God, and is under the power of the evil one (1 Jn 5:19). The devil inspires sin, not doing justice, and not loving brothers and sisters (1 Jn 3:8-10). It thus opposes key markers of the identity of the believing community. The world is also where the antichrists have gone after they "went out" from the authors and revealed that they did not belong to "us" (1 Jn 2:19). In not agreeing with the writer's Christology, they are judged to deny that Jesus is the Christ and the Father and the Son (1 Jn 2:22-3). The world is also inhabited by false prophets (1 Jn 4:1) and spirits who do not confess Jesus (1 Jn 4:2).

In this hostile context, the believing community is to be faithful in its identity and way of life, experiencing God's love, believing Jesus, abiding in God and Jesus, living in the presence of the Spirit, striving for perfection, knowing forgiveness for sin, living justice and love, surrounded by hostile powers, and destined for the life of the age.

Destined for "Life of the Age"

In addition to looking to the past to recall the beginning of the community's commitment to Jesus and God, and focusing on its present experiences and tasks, the speech also identifies a future component of the identity and way of life of community members. That future comprises the passing away of the world (the unbelieving Roman empire; 1 Jn 2:17), the return of Jesus (1 Jn 2:28), a day of judgment (1 Jn 4:17), transformation to be like Jesus (1 Jn 3:2-3), and the experience of eternal, or better, the life of the age (1:2; 2:17, 25; 3:15; 5:11-12, 13, 20). The speech offers no timetable or general schedule (cf. Mark 13). However, it should be noted that already in the present, the community participates in part in these future eschatological realities such as fellowship with God and Jesus, the forgiveness of sins, the presence of the Spirit. Already with the presence of the antichrists it is "the last hour" (2:18), which suggests the speech expects the end or goal of the divine purposes to be fully established soon. The writer is, of course, mistaken in this expectation.

The return or "coming" (*parousia*) of Jesus is described as a "revealing" (1 Jn 2:28). The speech does not describe the event (cf. Mt. 24:27-31) yet the word *parousia* evokes a cultural pattern of the display of dominant masculine power and rule by an emperor or victorious general or governor in entering a province or city. The writer presents Jesus's coming or *parousia* in imperial terms; the "savior of the world" (often used for emperors;

1 Jn 4:14) reveals the rule or dominating purposes of God which tolerate neither the injustices of the elite-benefitting Roman imperial system nor the dissent of non-believers.

Verse 28 focuses on the recipients' posture in welcoming his coming. By abiding in Jesus, they can be confident and not shamed because they encounter one who is familiar and who is their advocate, not one who condemns them. Moreover, in so doing they are enabled to live lives that imitate and embody God's love and thus have every reason for boldness rather than shame on the day of judgment ("as he is, so are we;" 1 Jn 2:17; 4:17).

By contrast, "the world" of Roman rule does not fare well (1 Jn 2:17). It, along with its "darkness (1 Jn 2:8), is passing away already; its destiny will be completed at the day of judgment (1 Jn 4:17; cf. 1 Cor. 7: 29-31). Marked by opposition to God and aligned with the devil, the world has not been given "life of the age." It is utterly incompatible with the divine purposes and with those who do the will of God. Its time has come to an end. Again, the speech does not dwell on how this "passing away" is to be accomplished or what, if anything, will replace it (compare Rev. 18–21).

The recipients are informed, though, that they will experience transformation to become like Jesus (1 Jn 3:2-3). Perhaps this expectation reflects that of John 5:27-9 concerning a general resurrection to either life or to condemnation for those who have done evil. Their present identity as God's children is affirmed along with the expectation of future change though the precise form or nature of that change is not clear. What the recipients can be assured of is that they will become like "him" and "see him as he is." Whether the "him" is God or Christ is not clear. The reference to being "children of God" at the beginning of verse 2 might suggest God is in view. The transformation cannot be something totally new. God is light and already the community walks in that light (1 Jn 1:5-7). God is love and already community members exhibit love (1 Jn 4:11-12). In preparation, however, community members are to purify themselves before the encounter with God (1 Jn 3:3).

The main emphasis in this future, eschatological expectation concerns the experience of "life of the age." This life is already known in the community of believers in fellowship with God (1 Jn 1:2-3), in abiding with the Father and the Son (1 Jn 2:25), in receiving God's gift in Jesus (1 Jn 5:11-12), and in believing in the Son of God (1 Jn 5:13, 20). It is not available for those who hate brothers and sisters, who are murderers (1 Jn 3:15) and who do not believe in the Son of God (1 Jn 5:12b). The writer excludes them from divine generosity.

The adjective often translated as "eternal" is better translated "life of the age" or "age-ly life." The phrase evokes a common, Jewish, eschatological understanding of at least two "ages" or periods of time marked by significantly different qualities of life. The current age features sin, death, the power of the devil, suffering, hostility, conflict, exploitative tyranny, and structures of oppression that cause poor quality of life for many people (war; food insecurity; disease; poverty; divisions and conflict, stress, shame, etc.). The coming new age removes all impediments to the experience of God and the accomplishment of the divine purposes. Its establishment ends sin, death, the devil, and oppression, and establishes good life for all including peace, abundant fertility and health (cf. 2 Bar. 72–4). The speech does not elaborate this life of the age in terms of these specifics. Central to its construction of life of the age is fellowship with God and Jesus, which is available in part now (1 Jn 1:2-3). This eschatological goal establishes in full the community's identity and way of life.

Conclusion

The speech employs important theological claims to underpin the identity and way of life that I identified in Chapter 6. These theological claims are not primarily checklists for intellectual assent but function pastorally to sustain the recipients' faithful living out of their identity and to distinguish them from outsiders. The identity is grounded in the loving actions of God who gives birth to community members. Members believe in and commit to Jesus as Christ and son or agent of God and receive his gifts including abiding in God and Jesus. They live in the presence of the Spirit. They strive for perfection yet they also sin; with confession they experience forgiveness. Their lives are to be marked by obedience to God's commandments, living justice and loving one another even as they are surrounded by hostile powers. And their goal and destiny at the return of Jesus is to be transformed and enter life of the age.

Part 3

2 and 3 John

8

2 John

Unlike 1 John, 2 and 3 John are clearly letters, employing a form well-known from Paul's letters and widely used in the ancient world.

Second John begins predictably with the writer identifying himself. Yet unlike Paul's letters, he neither gives his name (compare 1 Thess. 1:1a) nor explicitly describes his God-given identity as Paul does ("an apostle of Christ Jesus by the will of God," 2 Cor. 1:1a). He identifies himself only as "the elder." The term could identify the writer by age—an older man—or it could identify him with a title of ecclesial honor, authority, and leadership as the basis for addressing and instructing the recipients (Acts 20:17, 28, 1 Pet. 5:1). If both are in play, the title claims significant and superior authority over the recipients.

The term "elder" and the absence of a name raise another question. Does the relative anonymity of the term suggest that this figure is not a real person in a particular situation? Does the term suggest a fictional character in the narrative fiction who is constructed in order to convey authoritative-sounding instructions and warnings about the important question faced by numerous house-congregations, namely receiving itinerant teachers into house churches?

Immediately the elder names his recipients, the "elect lady and her children." As with himself, the writer does not name the lady or any of her "children." The anonymous term "lady" is respectful, perhaps a title of honor. It asserts leading status. This reverential address is reinforced by the flattering adjective "elect," which recognizes her as chosen by God (compare 1 Pet. 5:13). He uses the adjective to align the lady with himself.

Interpreters debate whether the title refers to a particular woman, is a collective term for a house-congregation or a fictional character that coheres with the fictional author to address the troubling situation of itinerant teachers. Female figures could represent (subjugated) peoples in the Roman empire. At the town of Aphrodisias in the province of Asia, for example, individual female figures represented numerous conquered peoples in carved statues in the approach to the imperial temple. And, after the defeat of Judea and destruction of Jerusalem and its temple in 70 CE, Rome celebrated and broadcast the victory with an image on Judea Capta coins ("Judea has been captured") that depicted Judea as a captured woman bound and kneeling before her captor, a hyper-masculine Roman soldier.

If the "lady" represents a people or group, the reference to "her children" fills out the group. Their presence constructs a household scene with the lady as the householder or leader of a house church and the "children" are believers who are members of this house-congregation (Philemon 2b). The writer's use of the term "children" asserts domination over them. Other women were church leaders such as Prisca (1 Cor. 16:19; Rom. 16:3-5a) and the nastily maligned woman leader of the church in Thyatira (Rev. 2:18-29).

The absence of a name for the addressee performs an important function. It does not confine the audience to one person or context. It encourages others to "read themselves into" the letter as its recipients. This anonymity reinforces the approach that the writer is constructing a fictional setting in order to provide general instruction concerning itinerant teachers.

More letter features follow. In verse 3 the writer greets the lady and her congregation, and in verse 4 celebrates that "some" of them are faithful. Verses 5-11 form the main body of the letter and state the letter's main purpose and content. The final verses (12-13) close out the letter with the conventions of naming a future visit from the elder-writer to the lady and her children, and the sending along of greetings from another group.

What Situation Does the Letter Address?

This is a difficult question to answer with certainty. The key issue is this: is 2 John addressed to a particular congregation and its specific circumstances, or is it a generalized letter that constructs a narrative fiction to address a common concern experienced by many congregations so as to instruct them how to react *if* and *when* the situation might arise? I incline more to the latter scenario but I recognize the first option is viable. And to add further complication, perhaps both options are in play.

In favor of the first scenario is the observation that Paul's letters conventionally address a particular community in particular circumstances. If this is true of 2 John, the writer addresses a particular situation with which he is familiar by exhorting the recipients to take a course of action and to refuse an alternative action. That is, he tries to persuade and dissuade, to encourage and discourage appropriate behavior. Yet in favor of the second option of a constructed narrative fiction is the invisibility of the writer-addressees, and the situation that the letter addresses which was a concern for numerous ecclesial groups (*Didache* 11–12). The letter comprises deliberative rhetoric in its efforts to persuade recipients to take particular actions in their situation.

The situation emerges most clearly in verses 7-11. The writer is concerned that people of whom he disapproves and whom he identifies as "deceivers" and "antichrist" have "gone out into the world." These people do not meet his Christological normativity: they "do not confess that Jesus Christ has come in the flesh." The language echoes 1 John 2:18-19 where the writer refers nastily to many antichrists who "went out from us" as "you," the recipients, have heard. These characters deny that "Jesus is the Christ" and "the Father and the Son" (1 Jn 2:22-3). The mark of 2 John's deceivers resembles those of 1 John with their focus on a Christological error. They "do not confess that Jesus Christ has come in the flesh" (2 Jn 7) whereas those of 1 John 2:18-19 deny Jesus is the Christ.

Yet the letter does not make an explicit connection with 1 John. And the wording of 2 John 7 differs somewhat from 1 John 2:18–19. Second John does not identify the origin of the deceivers as 1 John does. They have not gone out "from us." First John does not call them deceivers. Second John refers to one antichrist, not the "many antichrists" of 1 John 2:18.

Moreover, 2 John's descriptions are vague. Not only do the participants lack names and explicit roles, they also lack location. The writer says that the deceiving figures who do not share his and the lady's Christology exist "out into the world." This location is ideological or, more accurately, theological in that it stereotypically names what the writer deems to be a stance of opposition to God. It is not a geographical location. It indicates that deceiving teachers exist but it does not indicate that the deceiving teachers are nearby, nor does it suggest an imminent and urgent threat. The letter's orientation in verses 8-11 is to the future and to a *potential* and stereotypical situation. The letter's warning of the future arrival of deceiving itinerant teachers is not localized to a specific congregation (the lady's). Instead, it constructs a potential threat that might impact numerous congregations sometime in the future.

The letter, then, presents these congregations with a generic and generalized warning to "be on your guard" (2 Jn 8). Rather than understanding 2 John as being linked specifically to and a development of the scenario of those who "went out" in 1 John 2:18-19, 2 John seems to have a much broader horizon in view. It offers a general warning and instruction to many house congregations to be on the lookout for deceiving teachers and to refuse them an audience and hospitality.

This scenario of 2 John's address to numerous congregations about a widespread perception of possible and potential threats from itinerant deceiving teachers gains support from a further observation. Numerous writings from the early Jesus movement warn about the threat—real and/or imagined, actual and/or potential—that those whom they considered to be unauthorized and "outside" teachers posed to communities.

On one hand, in several letters, Paul faces specific and identifiable opponents active among those whom he addresses. In 2 Corinthians, he uses negative language to call them "false apostles, deceitful workers, disguising themselves as apostles of Christ" (2 Cor. 11:13). In Galatians, he accuses the other teachers of "bewitching" the Galatians (Gal. 3:1). In these instances, his addressees know whom he is attacking.

On the other hand, post-Paul, this scenario of Jesus-communities under threat from unidentified false teachers becomes a *topos* or a regular and generic feature in various writings. Numerous writings regularly included generalized warnings about potential deceivers without reference to specific opponents.

- Mark 13 issues a general warning for the time before Jesus's return: "Beware that no one leads you astray. Many will come in my name and say, 'I am he!' and they will lead many astray … False messiahs and false prophets will appear and produce signs and omens, to lead astray, if possible, the elect" (Mark 13:5-6, 22). The threat is future, potential, and general.
- Matthew's Gospel (Mt. 24:4-5, 11 "false prophets") and Luke's Gospel (Lk. 21:8) repeat this generic warning for the time period before Jesus's return.
- So too does John's Gospel. In a lengthy passage about Jesus the good shepherd caring for the sheep (followers), John's Jesus warns about "thieves and bandits" and "wolves" who will threaten the sheep/believers (John 10:7, 12). Second and 3 John do not use this language.

- The Paul of Acts 20:29 repeats the general and vague warning about unidentified wolves/opponents attacking the sheep/believers: "I know that after I have gone, savage wolves will come in among you, not sparing the flock."
- 2 Peter warns that "there will be false teachers among you, who will secretly bring in destructive opinions. They will even deny the Master …" (2 Pet. 2:1).
- 1 Timothy warns against deceiving teachers (1 Tim. 6:3-5).
- 2 Timothy also warns against deceiving teachers (2 Tim. 1:3-7; 3:13).
- 2 Thessalonians offers a general warning, "Let no one deceive you" (2 Thess. 2:3).
- Jude alerts its audience to intruding teachers that they have not recognized: "For certain intruders have stolen in among you, people who long ago were designated for this condemnation as ungodly, who pervert the grace of our God into licentiousness and deny our only Master and Lord, Jesus Christ" (Jude 1:4).

These warnings, found in numerous NT writings, function as identity-constructing and confirming statements. They secure the identity of the in-group of Jesus-followers by contrasting it not only with an out-group of deceiving teachers but with a hostile out-group that can damage the in-group's identity. The warnings affirm key commitments of the in-group that will be threatened by challenges from outsiders. The consequence of this contrast is that the in-group affirms and embraces even more tightly its identity-defining markers of ("true") belief and practice. The warnings function, then, not to provide "true and researched reporting" about an actual situation but to alert the recipients to a possible and potential threat to their group identity that causes them to affirm their identity more strongly.

Recognizing this identity-securing role does not mean that such opponents did not exist. The point of verses 7-11 is that *if* an itinerant teacher arrived at a congregation, the challenge for the group would be, says the writer, to identify whether the teacher was "true" or "false." The early Jesus movement did not have a process whereby ecclesial bodies ordained or credentialed approved teachers, missionaries, and leaders. There were no seminaries or theological schools issuing degrees, no internet to check out claims, no denominational boards credentialing vetted leaders.

Instead, one criterion by which house-congregations could assess itinerant teachers was by personal reference and letters of recommendation whereby a reputable figure guaranteed or commissioned a visiting teacher. For example, Paul commends Phoebe (Rom. 16:1), Timothy (1 Cor. 16:10), and Apollos (1 Cor. 16:12). In 2 Corinthians 3:1-2, Paul refers to the existence of the Corinthian believers as his letter of recommendation. This practice of personal endorsement is perhaps evident in 3 John 12 with its commendation of Demetrius who might be another missionary-teacher or might be the letter carrier. Second John with its anonymous writer and recipient does not employ this criterion.

Personal commendations, however, are not always possible. It was, then, the responsibility of congregations to recognize a "true" rather than "false" teacher. The writer of Revelation commends the church at Ephesus for having "tested those who claim to be apostles and are not and have found them to be false" (Rev. 2:2). But he does not say how they "tested" and "found" these "apostles" to be false.

A document from around 100 CE, the *Didache*, provides guidelines. It urges itinerant teachers to be welcomed but it identifies tests by which local house-congregations should assess true teachers.

- The teacher's teaching must be consistent with "everything mentioned above" and "bring righteousness and the knowledge of the Lord."
- If he teaches something different, "do not listen to him."
- If he stays "three days, he is a false prophet." And if "he asks for money, he is a false prophet." (*Didache* 11:1-6).

The author of the *Didache* provides three criteria by which a house-congregation can discern if an itinerant teacher is true or false. The teacher provides true (faithful and consistent) teaching, stays for a short time (less than three days) and without asking for money. If the teacher violates these criteria, the believers recognize a false teacher and must not listen to them.

Second John, then, belongs with other writings from around 100 CE in addressing a widely recognized concern to discern the credibility of visiting teachers. It constructs a scenario of "many deceivers [who] have gone out into the world" (2 Jn 7). It does not specify that these are the same "antichrists" of 1 John 2:18-19, though the name might be copied and these antichrists could form a subset of the "many deceivers." The language of "many deceivers" seems quite vague and generalizing. The letter does not evoke 1 John explicitly with language such as "as you know," or "as you remember."

Having named these deceivers and antichrist (2 Jn 7), 2 John issues a warning to the letter's recipients: "Be on your guard" (2 Jn 8). Verse 9 repeats the writer's key criterion for identifying a false teacher, namely discerning their Christological error. They do not "abide in the teaching about Christ." The writer allows for no diversity of belief.

The reference to "teaching" suggests a body of knowledge that has been taught and is definitive and authoritative. It suggests a more "fixed" entity than is evident in 1 John. Yet this teaching is not elaborated; presumably the recipients are assumed to know it and to agree with the elder. It marks them as insiders, the false or deceiving teachers as outsiders. Presumably the teaching concerns Jesus who has "come in the flesh," though that is surely only a part of it. Not knowing the true Christological teaching means that false teachers "do not have God." This verdict suggests that another element of the teaching affirms that Jesus reveals God and makes God known. Believing Jesus's identity results in having "both the Father and the Son," yet the precise nature of both the Christological error and "truth" remains general.

Verse 10 stipulates the response that the elder wants from whoever receives his letter. He instructs them to refuse these false teachers admission and hospitality. Such a snub exerts his authority and control as he maintains his normative Christology and does not tolerate any departure. He renders the false teachers voiceless; they are not allowed to speak because they do "not bring this teaching" about Jesus. And verse 10b adds a further reason for silencing and avoiding them. The false teachers are constructed, stereotypically, as performing "evil deeds." The writer assumes that moral deficiency inevitably accompanies false teaching. If the letter's recipients are receptive to false teaching, the writer claims, they will certainly fall prey to participating in evil deeds. The double threat of the false teachers is expressed in very general and stereotypical terms with which any house-community could identify.

I noted initially two possible scenarios for the address of 2 John and argued for my preference for understanding the letter as constructing a narrative fiction that addresses general audiences who might at some point experience the arrival of itinerant teachers and have to discern whether they are true or deceiving teachers. To be forewarned is to be forearmed.

The writer is faced with the challenge of persuading his recipients to follow his instruction to not welcome a false teacher into their house-assembly. How does he go about this persuasive task?

Persuasive Devices Employed by the Author

The persuasion begins in the opening verse with the writer's self-construction. As I have indicated, in identifying himself as "the elder," he evokes a cultural value of status and respect for older people as well as an ecclesial position of leadership and authority. He thus depicts himself as trustworthy and respectable yet authoritative.

Seeking to elicit the addressees' compliance and goodwill, he greets the recipients with two honorable terms, "lady" and "elect." Both terms express esteem. The first names a reputable social position and constructs her authority and leading position in the household and over her children. The second term affirms her theological identity in the divine purposes and as one of God's people. This recognition, perhaps flattery, allies the woman and her children with the writer and the divine purposes. This alliance matters because it locates this grouping on the "right" side of the binary that the writer will emphasize subsequently between true followers and deceivers. The greetings solicit the recipients' attention and readiness to hear his message.

He reinforces the alliance by declaring his love for them—the relative pronoun "whom" is plural—and aligning them three times with "the truth." In expressing love, he enacts a key community value and marker of "true" identity, namely love for one another, which he will emphasize by repetition in 2 John 5–6.

In naming "truth," he positions them as agreeing theologically with him and with God. This "truth" involves confessions about Jesus "come in the flesh" (2 Jn 7), abiding "in the teaching about Christ," and having both the Father and the Son" (2 Jn 7–9). He affirms them further by locating them in a broad circle of those "in the truth" who love them (2 Jn 1b). This circle probably involves "the children of your elect sister" whom he names as sending greetings in 2 John 13. Evoking them adds peer, familial, or community pressure to comply with the elder's teaching. The writer secures their identity in solidarity with "us" and in contrast to those who are not in the community defined by "the truth." The truth "abides in us" and not them. And its abiding guarantees the privileged eschatological destiny of writer and recipients since it is "with us forever" (2 Jn 2b).

The repeated use of "us" emphasizes the alliance and builds goodwill. So also does the threefold reference to truth, along with the subtle inference that not agreeing with the writer in denying welcome to false teachers would render recipients as not of "the truth" but aligned with "the false." The writer has affirmed their present identity with God, allied them with other believers, and acknowledged their future, certain destiny with God.

Verse 3 differs a little from the customary epistolary greeting. It has elements of an epistolary blessing in which the writer authoritatively positions himself as God's representative to confer divine gifts of "grace, mercy, and peace" on the recipients (compare Rom. 1:7b). The pleonastic designation for the divine ("God the Father and from Jesus Christ, the Father's Son") bolsters the writer's authority by association and agency. Yet the verse's wording—the statement begins with "it will be with us"—gives the benediction a sense of reassurance for the present and future for those allied with the writer and the lady.

Verse 2 ended with the declaration that truth "will be with us forever." With its future tense, verse 3 continues this emphasis on the future. The divine blessings continue into the future and ensure their eschatological destiny. Moreover, verse 3 retains the "us" pronoun from verse 2. Writer and recipients are allied as common beneficiaries of divine favor and are bound together in "truth and love." This is the fourth repetition of "truth" as an identifier of this divinely blessed alliance, and the second reference to love as a marker of the affection connecting writer and recipients. The wording of verse 3 underscores authority, goodwill, esteem, and alliance in aligning writer, recipients, God, and Jesus.

The writer expresses more esteem, solicits further goodwill, and builds the alliance by announcing delight that "some of your children" walk in the truth (2 Jn 4). The lady's children are explicitly aligned with the writer and the divine in the truth (the fifth time the noun is used) and affirmed to be obedient to God's command. The affirmation for the recipients here is strong yet the formulation expresses reserve. "Some" of the children are faithful; the partitive construction suggests that others are not. Some give no cause for joy.

The writer is not diverted to identify these others who are not faithful or address the causes or behaviors of their unfaithfulness. Rather, the reference is vague, suggestive, and sufficient for his persuasive purposes. The simple recognition of the unfaithful raises the possibility of vulnerability, that some can be drawn away from the truth. This recognition gains the recipients' attention and awareness that vulnerability must be protected. The subtle recognition prepares the way for the instruction to refuse admission to false teachers and missionaries in verses 10-11. They would draw some away from the truth.

A further persuasive technique develops this recognition of vulnerability by stating its consequences. The consequence of not being on guard is to damage or lose what "we have worked for" (2 Jn 8). The pronoun "we" not only binds writer and recipients but also places the recipients in a wider network of allied communities. But further is the risk of the loss of one's "full reward" and the loss of relationship with and blessing from God if one "does not abide in the teaching about Christ" (2 Jn 9). The threat of eschatological loss is again in view as in verse 2.

Verses 10-11 state the explicit command or prohibition that the writer's persuasive techniques have been preparing throughout to offer. To guard against vulnerability, false teachers are not to be welcomed into the house-congregation (2 Jn 10). Not only does their false teaching pose a threat, so too do their evil deeds (2 Jn 11). They are to be given no welcome, no hearing, no hospitality, no love.

The Limits of Love

The command to refuse welcome means withholding practical expressions of love in the form of welcome and hospitality from deceiving teachers. Yet love is a central practice for the letter's recipients and a marker of their identity. How does the writer maintain these two emphases?

In establishing their bond, the writer declares his love for the lady and her children in the opening verse. Significantly, in verses 5-6, he reminds his recipients of the old-new commandment, "let us love one another." The "we" language that recalls "we have had it from the beginning" draws writer and recipients together around this established tradition and puts the onus on the latter to (continue to) obey the love commandment. This obedience to the singular command means in verse 6 obeying the multiple commands of God through which love is expressed. This is the request the writer makes in verse 5, "I ask you (lady) . . . that you (lady and her children) walk in" these commandments expressing love.

The writer has strongly emphasized the importance of the love command. He reminds the recipients that "we" knew it from the beginning, the time of the initial reception of the proclamation about Christ and the resultant way of life. Love is expressed, he asserts, in God's commandments. And he asks for obedience—"walking"—according to the commandments. Taken together, verse 1, and verses 5-6 foreground the love command as *the* identifying mark and practice of his recipients who "walk in the truth" (2 Jn 4) and "have the Father and the Son" (2 Jn 9).

What, then, is the practice of love when deceiving teachers are "in the world," visiting believing communities, and requiring hospitality? How does the command to deny welcome align with the command to love? Among the commandments, for example, is that of Leviticus 19, which commands love for neighbors (19:18b), takes an expansive approach in urging provision for outsiders (Lev. 19:10), and urges "loving the alien as yourself" (19:33-4). These commands would seem to mandate welcome and hospitality for any in need.

Yet that is not what 2 John mandates. For the writer, "love" is an inside job.

In moving from its exhortation to love (2 Jn 5–6) to the discussion of what to do about itinerant teachers (2 Jn 7–11), the letter places boundaries on the practice of love that excludes deceiving teachers. The key to this move is the understanding of "one another." For 2 John, love extends only to those who share the writer's and recipients' Christological confession (2 Jn 7, 9). This confession constitutes "one another." Teachers who do not endorse that confession are not included in the "one another." They do not share "our" identity. They do not belong to and with "us." They are not embraced by either the love of God or the love of the house-congregation. The writer does not advocate extending love to those outside the community "in the world."

Second John's restriction of love only to those who think and act "like us" is consistent with 1 John's wondering as to how God's love could "abide in anyone who has the world's goods and sees a brother or sister in need and refuses help" (1 Jn 3:17). For these writers, the practice of love has boundaries. It is offered only to those who are brothers and sisters. It does not extend to deceiving teachers who do not share the writer-recipients' Christology and whose deeds are certain to be evil.

Conclusion

While 2 John employs features of a letter, its recipients are not clear. Is it written to a specific house congregation facing the imminent arrival of the deceiving teachers identified by 1 John? Or does it construct a narrative fiction that, like numerous other writings from the early Jesus movement, offers a general warning about the possible and potential arrival of false teachers who might threaten the recipient's identity? While both scenarios are possible, I have emphasized the second option. In urging house-groups not to receive itinerant, deceiving teachers, the writer employs numerous techniques to persuade recipients to obey his instruction. He clarifies that the love that marks the recipients' identity is for insiders only and is not to be extended to outsiders who are in the world.[1]

---

[1]In addition to various commentaries, two discussions have informed this chapter even though I dissent from some aspects of their analyses. Duane Watson, "A Rhetorical Analysis of 2 John According to Greco-Roman Convention," *New Testament Studies* 35 (1989): 104–30; Rikard Roitto, "Chapter 25: 2 John." In J. Brian Tucker and Aaron Kuecker (eds), *T & T Clark Social Identity Commentary on the New Testament* (London: T&T Clark, 2020), 567–70.

9

3 John

Like 2 John, and unlike 1 John, 3 John exhibits the features of a letter. This personal letter addresses Gaius and affirms his loyalty to the unnamed writer ("the elder") in carrying out his wishes by welcoming and provisioning some itinerant teachers. Using the rhetorical technique of *synkrisis*, the writer contrasts Gaius' commended action of welcome with a "bad guy," Diotrephes, who, according to the elder, did not welcome them. Unlike 2 John that addresses the "lady" in the singular in verses 1-5 before switching to the plural in verses 6 and following, 3 John remains addressed to Gaius throughout.

A Letter

Like the thirteen verses of 2 John, 3 John is also brief, with fifteen verses. Perhaps its brevity is determined by the size of the papyrus sheet on which it was written. And, like 2 John, it exhibits the standard features of a letter. It begins with the writer identifying himself not by name but by the title "elder." As with its use at the beginning of 2 John, the term could identify the writer by age—he is an older man—or it could identify him with a title of honor and authority appropriate to the ecclesial leadership role he claims in addressing and instructing Gaius (Acts 20:17, 28, 1 Pet. 5:1). If both are in play, the title claims significant authority.

It is not clear if this "elder" is the same figure who wrote 2 John. On one hand, this is possible. If so, he would be addressing an issue in one of the house-churches for which he asserts responsibility. As with 2 John, the issue concerns hospitality for visiting teachers and/or missionaries.

On the other hand, the title "elder" was not the exclusive possession of this one person. It features in a number of writings of the early Jesus movement to denote leaders of house-congregations.[1] For example:

---

[1] Acts 14:23; 15:2, 4, 6, 22-3; 20:17; 21:18; 1 Tim. 5:17, 19; Tit. 1:5; Jas 5:14; 1 Pet. 5:1, 5.

> And after they had appointed elders for them in each church, with prayer and fasting they entrusted them to the Lord.
>
> (Acts 14:23)

> Let the elders who rule well be considered worthy of double honor, especially those who labor in preaching and teaching;
>
> (1 Tim. 5:17)

> I left you behind in Crete for this reason, so that you should put in order what remained to be done, and should appoint elders in every town, as I directed you.
>
> (Tit. 1:5)

This widespread use of the title "elder" might suggest that the writer of 3 John is not the same leader who addresses a house-congregation in 2 John.

As with 2 John, the anonymity of "the elder" raises the question as to whether the letter reflects a particular house-church situation, or whether it constructs a narrative fiction comprising a generic situation with regard to visiting teachers providing general instruction to house-churches as to how they should receive visiting teachers. One clue that might support the latter position is that the named figures (Gaius, Demetrius, Diotrephes) represent different responses of which the writer approves and disapproves.

Verse 1b identifies the letter's recipient as Gaius. Clearly he is not "the Lady" of 2 John. His name is common and so allows readers to identify with him and the letter's address. Verses 2-4 express standard epistolary elements of a prayer for well-being (3 Jn 2), a commendation and common connections with the "brothers and sisters/friends"[2] (3 Jn 3–4). Verses 5-8 and 9-12 name the letter's central matter. The letter closes with more standard epistolary features. The writer expresses a desire to visit Gaius for face-to-face conversation (3 Jn 13–14), offers a benediction (3 Jn 15a), brings greetings from another group (3 Jn 15b), and greets others in Gaius' circle (3 Jn 15c).

---

[2]The Greek term literally means "brothers." Employing a more inclusive translation, the NRSV renders the term "friends." The intent is commendable but "friends" fails to express the household and kinship dimensions of the term. I have chosen to employ the rather clumsy "brothers and sisters/friends" phrase to express both a gender-inclusive translation and link it with the NRSV use of "friends." Given that 2 John addresses a woman as the house-congregation's leader, it is not unlikely to expect female missionaries.

What Situation Does the Letter Address?

For us, distanced from the letter's circumstances by some 2,000 years, whether those circumstances are a historical scenario or a narrative fiction, a number of elements, roles, and interactions remain elusive. Some clarity emerges in verses 6b-8 in particular; the following reconstruction of the scene's episodes before, in, and after the letter must remain tentative.

- The writer knows of itinerant visitors to Gaius' house-congregation (3 Jn 3–8). It is not clear if the elder sent them or allies with them. Either way he approves of them. Nor is it clear if Gaius is *the* leader or *a* leader of this house-congregation. The commendation for his actions in verses 6-8 suggests he is *the* leader but he is not formally identified as such. While the identity of the visitors is not clear in verse 3, verses 6b-8 indicate that they are likely itinerant teachers or missionaries.
- Gaius welcomed them to his house-congregation and supplied them with hospitality (accommodation, food) at some cost (3 Jn 5–8).
- These missionaries/teachers visited Diotrephes' house-congregation. According to the elder, by contrast, he refused to supply the visitors with hospitality and prevented others from doing so (3 Jn 9–10). It is not clear if Diotrephes and Gaius belong to the same house-congregation (co-leaders?). More likely, the scenario suggests each of them leads their own house-congregations. If this reconstruction is on target, the elder claims some supervision of both house-congregations.
- The itinerant missionaries returned to a house-assembly of which the elder might be the leader or at least has a physical presence. They testified to Gaius' "love" in supplying hospitality (3 Jn 3, 6).
- Presumably they also reported Diotrephes' opposition, his refusal to supply hospitality, and his general undermining of the elder's leadership (3 Jn 9–10).
- The writer has written a letter to "the church" (3 Jn 9). Which church is not stated. The most likely guess is that this is the church which Diotrephes leads. What does the letter say? We might imagine that in it the writer/elder asserts his authority and issues a public rebuke for Diotrephes. He urges the church to comply with the elder's instructions to provide hospitality for visiting missionaries. As far as we know, this letter has not survived.

- The writer writes the letter that we know as 3 John to Gaius outlining these events (3 Jn 1–8). The letter's pronouns and verbs are singular. The personal letter commends Gaius for his behavior, confirms it as appropriate, contrasts it with Diotrephes' behavior, and seeks to secure Gaius' continuing compliance and loyalty.
- The writer/elder evaluates Diotrephes' character and actions negatively since Diotrephes has defied the elder's wishes (3 Jn 9–10). He suggests he might visit Diotrephes and his house-congregation sometime. The visit will attempt to get Diotrephes in line (3 Jn 10).
- He also commends Demetrius, who may lead another house-congregation, or be an itinerant teacher/missionary, or be the one who delivers the letter to Gaius (3 Jn 12).
- The writer expresses hope for a face-to-face visit with Gaius "immediately" (3 Jn 14).

From this outline, it is clear that a number of interactions, episodes, and roles are not obvious to a modern audience. Yet there is some clarity about the basic situation. Whether a historical scenario or narrative fiction, the writer approves warmly of Gaius, who supplied hospitality for the visiting preachers/ missionaries, and is very disapproving of Diotrephes, who did not. The writer and Diotrephes are in a power struggle.

Relational and Positional Interactions

The Elder/Writer and Gaius

The writer's relationship with Gaius dominates the letter. Their geographical locations are not specified nor is their backstory elaborated. The elder is geographically distant from Gaius though he has heard about and approves of his actions in supporting the itinerants (3 Jn 3–8). He exerts some authority and expects compliance with his wishes, hence his being delighted with Gaius and disapproving of Diotrephes.

He recognizes Gaius as one of his children (3 Jn 4). Perhaps the elder had converted Gaius and other followers and brought them into "the truth." Or perhaps he sees himself as a father-figure in exercising authority and providing guidance and instruction for his house-congregation.

Despite recognizing these other "children," his attention is on Gaius. Five times he uses "love" language to express affection for Gaius. Four of these instances involve the adjective "beloved" used in the singular to refer only to Gaius. Beyond the initial descriptor of "beloved Gaius" in verse 1, the writer uses "beloved" three more times to address Gaius directly (3 Jn 2, 5, 11). In verse 1, he also uses the verb "love" to express his positive regard for and alliance with Gaius.

In addition to the "love" language, he employs the noun "truth" four times in the opening four verses. In verse 1, the writer declares his love for Gaius "in truth," suggesting his sincerity or genuineness. Thereafter, the noun applies to Gaius in commending him for his "faithfulness to the truth" and his "walking in the truth" (3 Jn 3–4). The verb "walk" is common language for living faithfully to the divine purposes (cf. Deut. 8:8; 10:12) so the elder praises Gaius for his obedient actions and way of life. Especially, that way of life involves providing hospitality for the visitors and so complying with the elder's wishes (3 Jn 5–8). The elder also affirms Gaius to be "faithful" (3 Jn 5).

Yet in verse 8, the term "truth" seems to have a broader meaning. Assuming the visitors are teachers or missionaries, the writer affirms Gaius's support for them and those like them as an opportunity to be "co-workers with the truth." Here "truth" seems to refer to the proclamation of the Gospel message and supporting the mission of spreading the Gospel.

In addition, the elder twice expresses his emotions of "joy" in relation to Gaius' actions of extending hospitality. The elder is "overjoyed" to hear a report from the "brothers and sisters/friends" (lit., 3 Jn 3). And he expresses himself as having "no greater joy" in hearing of such actions by his "children" (3 Jn 4).

This language of "love," "truth," "faithfulness," and "joy" expresses the writer's positive disposition toward Gaius, reinforces and augments the existing goodwill he feels toward him, and seeks to secure Gaius' continuing compliance and alliance with the writer. Assuming the writing constructs the fiction of the elder with oversight over several house-congregations, he links Gaius to his other "children" or believers who also walk in the truth (3 Jn 4). Perhaps the backstory is that the elder converted them; perhaps he understands multiple house-congregations to comprise one large household or family under his supervision. However we understand his "children" who "walk in truth," this larger context exerts subtle pressure on Gaius to continue to be loyal to the elder, and to not lose face by being led astray by Diotrephes.

While verses 1-4 have emphasized the writer/elder's affection for Gaius, they have not told us much about Gaius beyond his compliance with the elder's wishes. The elder warmly approves of him. The "brothers and sisters/ friends" have made an appreciative and positive report about his faithfulness and love (3 Jn 3, 6). But what has Gaius done? And what is his position or function?

The letter does not explicitly clarify his position. The best guess is that he is either the leader of a house-congregation under the elder's oversight, or a patron of such a group. It does not seem to be the same group as that of Diotrephes. More details about his actions emerge in verses 5-8.

The main reason for the elder's commendation of Gaius is his treatment of the "friends" or "brothers and sisters/friends," "even though they are strangers to you" (3 Jn 5). The relationship of these "brothers and sisters/ friends" to the elder is not clear. He does not claim to have sent them, though he has heard their report of Gaius' faithfulness "before the church" (3 Jn 3, 6). By calling them "brothers and sisters/friends" and noting their positive report, he aligns himself with them and aligns Gaius both with himself and them.

Gaius has helped them but the elder is vague initially about what he did. He "spiritualizes" Gaius' contribution first as expressions of "walking in the truth" and then "love" (3 Jn 3, 6). Verse 5 is equally vague: "whatever you do for" them. More details emerge in verse 6b. The verb "to send them on/ forward" is commonly used with reference to preachers and missionaries setting off on mission journeys (Acts 15:3; 21:5; 1 Cor. 16:6, 11; 2 Cor. 1:16).

For example, Paul writes to the church in Rome:

> I desire, as I have for many years, to come to you when I go to Spain. For I do hope to see you on my journey and to be sent on by you, once I have enjoyed your company for a little while.
>
> (Rom. 15:23-4)

Paul does not expect from the believers in Rome prayer and a pep talk. Rather, "being sent on" means supplying finance, food, transport, connections, and letters of recommendation for his mission work as he travels from Rome to Spain. The mission discourse in Matthew 10:9-11 instructs disciples to rely on "worthy houses" for supplies and hospitality, "for laborers deserve their food." And Titus 3:13 gives this instruction:

> Make every effort to send Zenas the lawyer and Apollos on their way, and see that they lack nothing.
>
> (Tit. 3:13)

To lack nothing suggests supplying finances and whatever material goods missionaries needed.

The writer recognizes that Gaius has "sent them on" (3 Jn 6a). He has supplied them with necessary provisions as expressions of his "love" and "faithfulness." Perhaps he hosted them in his house while they stayed in his area as well as supplied provisions and funds for the next stage of their journey. These acts of hospitality indicate that Gaius is a person of some resources that he has used for the benefit of the missionaries.

The writer offers a double affirmation for Gaius and his action. His act of self-giving is "worthy of God" (3 Jn 6b). And he is an example to other believers. Since the visitors are journeying "for the sake of Christ," it is up to Christ-believers like Gaius to do their duty and offer this sort of material support since missionaries do not rely on unbelievers or outsiders (3 Jn 7). Having held Gaius up as a model, the elder then generalizes Gaius' practices. He has done what "we ought" to do to be coworkers with these missionaries who walk in the truth (3 Jn 8). Just who the elder has in mind as an audience for this generalizing comment is not clear. Perhaps "we" refers to the elder and Gaius. Perhaps he hopes that other believers will read the letter.

The Elder/Writer and Diotrephes

In verses 9-10, the writing employs the rhetorical technique of *synkrisis,* or comparison, to construct a contrast with Gaius in the figure of Diotrephes. As with Gaius, he does not explicitly name his relationship with Diotrephes nor identify the latter's role. Given the writer/elder's level of concern, it seems that the church to which he writes (3 Jn 9) is separate from Gaius' church and from the church immediately associated with the elder to which the missionaries testified about Gaius (3 Jn 3, 6). A reasonable guess is that Diotrephes is the leader of another house-congregation to which the missionaries have traveled. The elder/writer has, or claims to have, some oversight over the churches of both Gaius and of Diotrephes.

The elder/writer does not tell Gaius what he wrote in his letter to Diotrephes' church (3 Jn 9), but he *does* tell Gaius what he thinks of Diotrephes. He levels five charges against Diotrephes.

1   He claims Diotrephes "likes to put himself first" or claim preeminence or the first rank (3 Jn 9b). The Greek word appears only here in the New Testament. It draws together two words "love" and "being first." Plutarch roots this desire in "selflove (which) makes men eager to be first and to be victorious in everything" (*Moralia,* "On Tranquility of Mind," 471D). This desire to be dominant suggests eliminating any challenger. It is typical of the mindset and behavior of hegemonic

masculinity in the ancient world, whereby elite males competed for societal and political dominance over each other and non-elites. The elder's disapproving charge is that Diotrephes is embodying this behavior in relation to him and the house-congregation.

2 The elder's second charge against Diotrephes develops the first and heightens the power struggle between them. The translation of the verb is controversial since the two uses of this (prefixed) verb in verses 9 and 10 are its only uses in the NT. Elsewhere in the NT the verb (with and without other prefixes) refers to welcoming or receiving itinerants. In Rom. 16:2, Paul commends Phoebe to his readers so that "you may welcome her in the Lord." In 2 Cor. 7:15, Paul refers to Titus' recollection of "how you (the Corinthians) welcomed him." In Acts 17:7, one of the believers, Jason, "has entertained [Paul and Silas] as guests." The verb occurs six times in Matt. 10:40-1 to refer to the welcome extended to missionaries but with the extra claim by the Matthean Jesus that "whoever welcomes you, welcomes me." The "welcome" of itinerants in these mission contexts indicates providing them with hospitality and supplies. The elder's claim in 3 Jn 9b is that Diotrephes has not welcomed him, whether in person on previous visit(s) or whether in the form of the missionaries with whom the elder closely identifies. The writer accuses Diotrephes of not providing hospitality including accommodation, food and finance. To reject them is to reject him. To dishonor them is to dishonor him.

3 The elder's third charge involves what he will say if he visits Diotrephes. "I will remind him about the works he does in evil words as he talks nonsense about/brings unjustified charges against us" (lit., 3 Jn 10a). The challenge for translation is that this is another verb used only here in the New Testament. Possible translations are that Diotrephes "talks nonsense about" or that he is "spreading false charges against us" (NRSV). The writer does not specify what the "nonsense" is or what the "unjustified charges" might be. Nor is it clear who are the "us" about whom nonsense is being spoken: the elder, the missionaries, the elder's church, Gaius?

4 The fourth charge expands the second charge. Not only does Diotrephes not welcome and supply hospitality for the elder, he does not welcome and provide hospitality for the visiting missionaries, the brothers and sisters or friends (3 Jn 10b). He does not do what Gaius does.

5 The fifth charge attacks Diotrephes' leadership and negative impact on the house-congregation. Not only does he not provide for the

missionaries, but he prevents others doing so and expels them from the church (3 Jn 10c). The elder asserts that some in Diotrephes' church resisted his practice of not supplying hospitality and tried to obey the elder's wishes to do so. Church members are thus caught up in the power struggle between the elder and Diotrephes with, so the elder claims, the latter forcing some to defy the elder. The elder blames Diotrephes for splitting the group. And he claims that Diotrephes casts out those who do not agree with him. This is a condemning claim. Threatening and expelling those whom he considers non-compliant enacts poor leadership. A better strategy would be to seek understanding, relationship, and inclusion. Diotrephes fails to recognize that they perform the "love," "truth," and "faithfulness" that Gaius performs and that brings joy to the elder.

Throughout, we do not get Diotrephes' perspective on the situation or on the elder. Nor is it clear what the elder plans to do about this situation. In 3 Jn 10, he contemplates visiting Diotrephes ("if I come") but does not commit to doing so. *If* he does visit, he says that he "will remind" Diotrephes of these five grievances. The verb "remind" denotes a low-key intervention. He does not plan to confront or rebuke or punish or expel Diotrephes. He does not label him with the language for opponents that 1 and 2 John use—"false prophet," "antichrist," or "deceiver"—nor does he charge him with "going out from us" (1 Jn 2:19) or "going out into the world" (2 Jn 7). Perhaps this restraint indicates a desire more for reconciliation than punishment. Or perhaps it demonstrates that the elder does not have as much authority over Diotrephes in reality as he would like and as he seems to imply in his words.

Having targeted Diotrephes, he addresses Gaius directly in 3 John 11. For the fifth time he expresses his love for Gaius, and for the first time gives him a direct command. He is not to imitate evil but imitate what is good. In context, the command requires Gaius to choose between Diotrephes, who exemplifies the evil of not supplying hospitality, and the elder's teaching to supply hospitality. But further in 3 John 11b, in making this decision, the elder increases the pressure on Gaius and sets a test before him. His decision for "doing the good"—aligning with the elder and supplying missionaries with hospitality—will disclose whether he is "from God" or not. His decision for "doing evil"—aligning with Diotrephes and not providing hospitality— will reveal that he has not "seen God." At stake, according to the elder, is not just Gaius' political-ecclesial allegiance but Gaius' relationship with or against God.

The appeal is rather strange given the effusive praise the elder offers to Gaius in verses 1-8 for offering hospitality to the missionaries. Verse 11 may say more about the elder than Gaius. It suggests that the elder is not nearly as confident in Gaius as that initial passage suggests. Now he constructs Gaius as somewhat fickle and vulnerable to the influence of Diotrephes. In making such a freighted appeal to Gaius, the elder also reveals he is not confident in his own authority and leadership to maintain Gaius' loyalty.

The Elder and Demetrius

In verse 12, suddenly another figure comes to the fore. There are no other references to Demetrius. Presumably he is introduced as another of the elder's favored children in alliance with Gaius and in contrast to Diotrephes.

Since the letter does not elaborate Demetrius' identity, interpreters have made various guesses. Perhaps he was a member of Diotrephes' church and, in contrast to Diotrephes, welcomed the missionaries. Perhaps he is a well-attested, itinerant missionary. Perhaps he is one of the "brothers and sisters/ friends" who reported to the elder on Gaius and Diotrephes and the elder mentions him as the reliable source for his attack on Diotrephes (3 Jn 3). Perhaps he is the leader of another house-congregation under the elder's supervision and the elder mentions him as another ally for Gaius and against Diotrephes. Perhaps he is the one who carries the elder's letter to Gaius and the elder vouches for him so Gaius will take the letter seriously.

A case can be made for all these options and interpreters have their favorites. But ultimately, we do not know. It seems, though, that at least Demetrius serves the elder's purpose of securing Gaius' loyalty and continuing practice of offering hospitality.

Whatever Demetrius' role, the elder parades his virtuous qualities before Gaius. First, the elder's claim that "everyone" speaks positively about Demetrius exerts pressure on Gaius to align with this majority against Diotrephes. Second, the elder's presentation of Demetrius in relation to "truth" shows Gaius that Demetrius, like him and unlike Diotrephes, is "faithful to the truth" and "walks in the truth" (3 Jn 3) and is a "co-worker with the truth" (3 Jn 8). Third, the elder explicitly adds his testimony about Demetrius' quality. The language of "you know" and the claim of the truth of the elder's testimony emphasize the perspective that the elder wants Gaius to embrace.

Verse 12, like verse 11, suggests that the elder is not confident in Gaius' allegiance despite his claims of verses 1-8. He seems to be very worried about Gaius' vulnerability to Diotrephes' influence. He works hard in verses 11-12 to secure Gaius' allegiance and "true" practice of welcoming missionaries with hospitality.

Concluding the Letter

The elder ends the letter with several epistolary conventions. The first, in verses 13-14, anticipates a future meeting with Gaius. The elder says he has much more to write but prefers a future face-to-face meeting with Gaius. In keeping with the other instances of imprecisions in the letter, he does not say whether he intends to visit Gaius or whether Gaius should visit him.

Verse 15 employs the convention of extending greetings. He sends peace to Gaius. The sending of peace is not unique in NT writings.

> Peace be to the whole community, and love with faith, from God the Father and the Lord Jesus Christ.
>
> (Eph. 6:23)

> Peace to all of you who are in Christ.
>
> (1 Pet. 5:14)

And in John's Gospel, post-resurrection, the Johannine Jesus extends peace to the disciples.

> Peace be with you.
>
> (Jn 20:19, 21)

Like the rest of 3 John, the writer does not link his sending of peace with any theological or Christological statements.

A second sending of greetings involves "the friends" (*philoi*) sending greetings to Gaius. This too is a feature of Jesus-movement letters. For example, Paul sends along greetings from various people:

> Timothy, my co-worker, greets you; so do Lucius and Jason and Sosipater, my relatives. I Tertius, the writer of this letter, greet you in the Lord. Gaius, who is host to me and to the whole church, greets you. Erastus, the city treasurer, and our brother Quartus, greet you.
>
> (Rom. 16:21-3)

Again, reflecting other imprecisions in the letter, the writer does not identify who these "friends" might be.

And third, the elder ends the letter by again appealing to a wider community and instructing Gaius to "greet the friends there." The evoking of these friends continues the elder's concern to corral Gaius into remaining faithful to the elder and his wishes.

Evaluation

Third John makes no theological arguments. Theological issues do not seem to matter in its endorsements of Gaius and Demetrius and opposition to Diotrephes. It invokes "truth" but leaves the notion undefined.

The letter's emphasis is complying with the elder's practice of extending hospitality (funds, accommodation, provisions) to itinerant missionaries. In this regard, a comparison with 2 John is interesting.

Second John is suspicious of itinerant teachers and missionaries. "Many deceivers" are abroad (2 Jn 7). Their defining mark is errant Christological teaching (2 Jn 7b–9). So the elder urges the house-congregation to be alert (2 Jn 8) and not to welcome any itinerant with errant christology "into the house" (2 Jn 10–11).

Third John does not exhibit this suspicion. The elder seems to think that itinerant missionaries and teachers should automatically be welcomed with hospitality. The elder praises Gaius for supplying itinerant missionaries with hospitality "even though they are strangers to you" (3 Jn 5). It is surprising that they were "strangers" (*xenous*) to Gaius and that Gaius nevertheless welcomed them since letters of commendation and networks of contacts were available to verify strangers. The elder does not mention the origin of these missionaries. He does not claim to have sent them so they do not come to Gaius with the elder's commendation. In fact, it is not clear that the elder knew of their mission until they return to testify about Gaius in the house-congregation (3 Jn 3). And he is silent about endorsing their Christology, apart from a general nod to "the truth" (3 Jn 8).

Among the elder's commendation for Gaius, there is no commendation that Gaius has verified the claims of the itinerant missionaries to be "true." Gaius is commended for supporting them but not for the alertness and verification of itinerants that 2 John requires.

Even though the elder berates him, perhaps Diotrephes is closer to 2 John's alertness when he refuses hospitality to the missionaries. Perhaps Diotrephes was concerned with the missionaries' teaching and did not find their Christology acceptable. Perhaps he was concerned that they arrived without a letter of commendation. Or if they did happen to have some commendation from the elder, perhaps Diotrephes did not trust the elder because of previous encounters. Perhaps he does nor recognize that the elder has any authority to tell Diotrephes what to do, however the elder constructs and asserts himself. Or perhaps he regarded all itinerants as threats, and being "alert" and suspicious, he refused admission to all and any. We do not know.

But it certainly does not suit the elder's purpose to present Diotrephes in a positive light for his approach to itinerant missionaries. Five accusations discredit him and his practices as the elder asserts his power in the hope of cementing Gaius' loyalty.

Demetrius offers another variant, whatever his role. Others speak well of him. And the elder endorses him. If he carries the letter to Gaius, or if he is an itinerant himself, verse 12 functions as his endorsement. Perhaps the "brothers and sisters/friends" carried a similar endorsement in their mission activity. We do not know.

Generally, 3 John does not appear to be nearly as concerned with identifying and credentialing itinerants as 2 John. Third John's emphasis is on the responsibility of providing hospitality. The elder asserts this responsibility, praising and affirming Gaius for doing so, attacking Diotrephes for not doing so, and commending Demetrius as worthy of such hospitality. And throughout the letter the elder asserts his authority, though its basis whether personal charisma, some social status and resources, previous "fatherly" missionary activity that produced communities of "children," or his ability to build networks, is not clear.

His continual efforts to bind Gaius to himself, his reticence to confront Diotrephes ("if I come," 3 Jn 10) and Diotrephes' willingness to defy his wishes, might attest the unstable basis for and exercise of his authority.

It is not clear whether 3 John addresses an actual, local, particular, historical situation or whether it constructs a narrative fiction to encourage a widespread acceptance of itinerants. Whichever scenario interpreters adopt, and I tend to the latter, the writing employs its cast of characters—the elder, Gaius, Diotrephes, Demetrius—to persuade recipients to welcome itinerant teachers into their ecclesial communities.

Select Bibliography

Balch, David. "Two Apologetic Encomia: Dionysius on Rome and Josephus on the Jews," *Journal for the Study of Judaism* 13 (1982): 102–22.

Black, C. Clifton. "The First, Second, and Third Letters of John. Introduction, Commentary, and Reflections." In *The New Interpreter's Bible*, edited by Leander E. Keck, 12.363–469. Nashville: Abingdon, 1998.

Brooke, A. E. *A Critical and Exegetical Commentary on the Johannine Epistles.* Edinburgh: T&T Clark, 1912.

Brown, Raymond E. *The Community of the Beloved Disciple: The Life, Loves and Hates of an Individual Church in New Testament Times.* New York: Paulist, 1979.

Brown, Raymond E. *The Epistles of John.* Anchor Bible 30. Garden City: Doubleday, 1982.

Carter, Warren. *What Does Revelation Reveal? Unlocking the Mystery.* Nashville: Abingdon, 2011.

Coombes, Malcolm. "A Different Approach to the Structure of I John." *Australian eJournal of Theology* 14 (2009): 1–30.

Culpepper, R. Alan. *John, the Son of Zebedee: The Life of a Legend*, 89–95. Columbia: University of South Carolina Press, 1994.

Culpepper, R. Alan, and Paul N. Anderson (eds.). *Communities in Dispute: Current Scholarship on the Johannine Epistles.* Society of Biblical Literature Early Christianity and Its Literature 13. Atlanta: SBL, 2014.

Dodd, C. H. *The Johannine Epistles.* London: Hodder & Stoughton, 1946.

Friesen, Steven. "Poverty in Pauline Studies: Beyond the So-Called New Consensus." *Journal for the Study of the New Testament* 26 (2004): 322–61.

Griffith, Terry. "A Non-Polemical Reading of 1 John: Sin, Christology and the Limits of Johannine Christianity." *Tyndale Bulletin* 49.2 (1998): 253–76.

Häring, Theodor. "Gedankengang und Grundgedanke des ersten Johannesbriefes," in *Theologische Abhandlungen Carl von Weizächer gewidmet*, 171–200. Freiburg: Mohr, 1892.

Hills, Julian V. "A Genre for 1 John. In *The Future of Early Christianity*, edited by Birgir A. Pearson, 367–77. Minneapolis: Fortress, 1991.

Houlden, J. L. *A Commentary on The Johannine Epistles.* Peabody: Hendrickson, 1973.

Jensen, Matthew D. "The Structure and Argument of 1 John: A Survey of Proposals." *Currents in Biblical Research* 12 (2014): 194–215.

Jones, Peter R. *1, 2, & 3 John*. Macon: Smyth & Helwys, 2009.

Kysar, Robert. "John, Epistles Of." In *The Anchor Bible Dictionary*, III, edited by David Noel Freedman, 900–12. New York: Doubleday, 1992.

Lampe, Peter. "The Roman Church of Romans 16." In *The Romans Debate*, edited by Karl P. Donfried, 216–30. Grand Rapids: Baker Academic, 1977, 1991, 2005.

Law, Robert. *The Tests of Life: A Study of the First Epistle of St. John*. Edinburgh: T&T Clark, 1909.

Lieu, Judith M. *The Second and Third Epistles of John: History and Background*. Edinburgh: T&T Clark, 1986.

Lieu, Judith M. *The Theology of the Johannine Epistles*. Cambridge: Cambridge University Press, 1991.

Lieu, Judith M. *I, II, & III John: A Commentary*. Louisville: Westminster John Knox, 2008.

Lieu, Judith M. "Us or You? Persuasion and Identity in 1 John." *Journal of Biblical Literature* 127 (2008): 805–19.

Judith Lieu, "The Audience of the Johannine Letters." *Communities in Dispute: Current Scholarship on the Johannine Epistles*, edited by R. Alan Culpepper and Paul N. Anderson, 123–40. Atlanta: SBL, 2014.

Malatesta, Edward. *The Epistles of St. John. Greek Text and English Translation Schematically Arranged*. Rome: Pontifical Gregorian University, 1973.

Marshall, I. Howard. *The Epistles of John*. The New International Commentary on the New Testament. Grand Rapids: Eerdmans, 1978.

Mitchell, Margaret. "'Diotrephes does not receive us': The Lexicographical and Social Context of 3 John 9–10." *Journal of Biblical Literature* 117 (1998): 299–320.

Mitchell, Margaret. "John, Letters Of." In *The New Interpreter's Dictionary of the Bible*, edited by Katharine Doob Sakenfeld, 3.370–4. Nashville: Abingdon, 2008.

O'Day, Gail. "1, 2, and 3 John." In *Women's Bible Commentary*, edited by Carol A. Newsom and Sharon H. Ringe, 466–7. Louisville: Westminster John Knox, 1998.

Painter, John. "The 'Opponents' in 1 John." *New Testament Studies* 32 (1986): 48–71.

Painter, John. *1, 2, and 3 John*. Sacra Pagina 18. Collegeville: Liturgical Press, 2002.

Rensberger, David. *1 John, 2 John, 3 John*. Abingdon New Testament Commentaries. Nashville: Abingdon, 1997.

Roitto, Rikard. "Practices of Confession, Intercession, and Forgiveness in 1 John 1:9; 5:16." *New Testament Studies* 58 (2012): 232–53.

Roitto, Rikard. "Identity in 1 John: Sinless Sinners who Remain in Him." In *T&T Clark Handbook to Social Identity in the New Testament*, edited by J. Brian Tucker and Aaron Kuecker, 493–510. London: T&T Clark, 2014.

Roitto, Rikard. "Chapter 24: 1 John." In *T&T Clark Social Identity Commentary on the New Testament*, edited by J. Brian Tucker and Aaron Kuecker, 555–66. London: T&T Clark, 2020.

Roitto, Rikard. "Chapter 25: 2 John." In *T&T Clark Social Identity Commentary on the New Testament*, edited by J. Brian Tucker and Aaron Kuecker, 567–70. London: T&T Clark, 2020.

Roitto, Rikard. "Chapter 26: 3 John." In *T&T Clark Social Identity Commentary on the New Testament*, edited by J. Brian Tucker and Aaron Kuecker, 571–3. London: T&T Clark, 2020.

Russell, D. A., and N. G Wilson, *Menander Rhetor, Edited with Translation and Commentary*. Oxford: Clarendon, 1981.

Schnackenburg, Rudolf. *The Johannine Epistles: Introduction and Commentary*. New York: Crossroad, 1992.

Segovia, F. "Recent Research in the Johannine Letters." *Religious Studies Review* 13 (1987): 132–9.

Smith, D. Moody. *First, Second, and Third John*. Interpretation. Louisville: John Knox Press, 1991.

Smith, D. "The Epistles of John: What's New Since Brooke's ICC in 1912?" *Expository Times* 120.8 (2009); 373–84.

van Staden, P. J. "The Debate on the Structure of 1 John." *Hermorde Theological Studies* 47: (1991) 487–502.

Streett, Daniel R. *They Went Out From Us: The Identity of the Opponents In First John*. Berlin: de Gruyter, 2011.

Sugirtharajah, R. S. "The First, Second and Third Letters of John." In *A Postcolonial Commentary on the New Testament Writings*, edited by Fernando R. Segovia and R. S. Sugirtharajah, 413–23. London: T&T Clark, 2007.

von Wahlde, Urban. *The Johannine Commandments: I John and the Struggle for the Johannine Tradition*. New York: Paulist, 1990.

Watson, Duane F. "A Rhetorical Analysis of 2 John According to Greco-Roman Convention." *New Testament Studies* 35 (1989): 104–30.

Watson, Duane F. "A Rhetorical Analysis of 3 John: A Study in Epistolary Rhetoric." *Catholic Biblical Quarterly* 51 (1989): 479–501.

Watson, Duane F. "1 John 2:12–14 as *Distributio, Conduplicatio,* and *Expolitio*: A Rhetorical Understanding." *Journal for the Study of the New Testament* 35 (1989): 97–110.

Watson, Duane F. "Amplification Techniques in 1 John: The Interaction of Rhetorical Style and Invention." *Journal for the Study of the New Testament* 51 (1993): 99–123.

Westcott, Brooke F. *The Epistles of St John: The Greek Text with Notes and Essays*. Cambridge: Macmillan and Co. 1892.

Author Index

Subject Index